DESIRING THE DEAD
NECROPHILIA AND NINETEENTH-CENTURY FRENCH LITERATURE

THE EUROPEAN HUMANITIES RESEARCH CENTRE

UNIVERSITY OF OXFORD

The European Humanities Research Centre of the University of Oxford organizes a range of academic activities, including conferences and workshops, and publishes scholarly works under its own imprint, LEGENDA. Within Oxford, the EHRC bridges, at the research level, the main humanities faculties: Modern Languages, English, Modern History, Classics and Philosophy, Music and Theology. The Centre stimulates interdisciplinary research collaboration throughout these subject areas and provides an Oxford base for advanced researchers in the humanities.

The Centre's publishing programme focuses on making available the results of advanced research in medieval and modern languages and related interdisciplinary areas. An Editorial Board, whose members are drawn from across the British university system, covers the principal European languages. Titles currently include works on Arabic, Catalan, Chinese, English, French, German, Italian, Portuguese, Russian, Spanish and Yiddish literature. In addition, the EHRC co-publishes with the Society for French Studies, the Modern Humanities Research Association and the British Comparative Literature Association. The Centre also publishes a Special Lecture Series under the LEGENDA imprint, and a journal, *Oxford German Studies*.

Enquiries about the Centre's academic and publishing programme
should be addressed to:
European Humanities Research Centre
University of Oxford
76 Woodstock Road, Oxford OX2 1HP
enquiries@ehrc.ox.ac.uk
www.ehrc.ox.ac.uk

LEGENDA

European Humanities Research Centre
University of Oxford

Desiring the Dead

Necrophilia and Nineteenth-Century French Literature

LISA DOWNING

LEGENDA

European Humanities Research Centre
University of Oxford
2003

Published by the
European Humanities Research Centre
of the University of Oxford
47 Wellington Square
Oxford OX1 2JF

LEGENDA is the publications imprint of the
European Humanities Research Centre

ISBN 1 900755 65 3

First published 2003

British Library Cataloguing in Publication Data
A CIP catalogue record for this book is available from the British Library

LEGENDA series designed by Cox Design Partnership, Witney, Oxon
Printed in Great Britain by
Information Press
Eynsham
Oxford OX8 1JJ

Copy-Editor: Polly Fallows

CONTENTS

THIS BOOK IS DEDICATED TO THE MEMORY OF K.R.W.
THAT IT MAY REST IN PEACE

ACKNOWLEDGEMENTS

I would firstly like to thank Malcolm Bowie, Michael Moriarty and Ritchie Robertson for demonstrating their belief in this project and acting to ensure its publication. I want also to record my immense gratitude to Margaret Whitford, who introduced me to the field of psychoanalytic thought as an undergraduate, and who, as my colleague at Queen Mary, University of London, continues to provide me with regular doses of insight, wisdom and good judgement.

Warm thanks are due to the many colleagues, friends and students who have offered encouragement and help with this project, from conceptualization to completion, especially: Emily Baldock, Colin Davis, Fiona Handyside, Samantha Jordan, Katherine Lunn-Rockcliffe, Edward Nye, Stefan Pollan, Christopher Robinson, Gerard Ruitenberg, Dena Ryness, Pria Taneja, Ingrid Wassenaar and Edward Welch. I am particularly indebted to Robert Gillett and Josep-Anton Fernàndez, my co-teachers on the Gay and Lesbian Studies course at QMUL, who have taught me so much about the discursive traps into which we risk falling when we talk and write about sexuality.

Finally, to Ben, to Dany, and to Sheila and John, I acknowledge my immense personal debt. In offering me their own unique kinds of friendship, love, sustenance and belief, they have been tireless.

INTRODUCTION

De toutes les anomalies qui frappent et révèlent le genre humain, la nécrophilie est assurément celle qui fait le plus horreur aux peuples civilisés dès qu'elle se produit.

HUBERT JUIN[1]

The Nature of the Necrophile

There is a rather puerile pun in the English language, to which I have been frequently subjected when telling acquaintances about the topic of this book for the first time. It goes something like 'necrophilia—it's dead boring'. The form of this pun is telling. 'Dead boring' is amusingly bathetic, suggesting that this extreme and shocking sexual perversion may not, in fact, be a very stimulating one for the perpetrator. Simultaneously, the second and literal meaning of 'boring' euphemistically evokes the act most readily suggested by the term 'necrophilia'—that of sexual intercourse with the dead (implicitly, by means of male penetration of a female corpse). This *jeu de mot* is accurate and concise, then, in its summing up of some of the stereotypical ideas surrounding necrophilia. Moreover its function—to make us laugh at something frightening and extreme—is itself suggestive, following the Freudian logic that jokes may work to diffuse the power of, and thereby make safe, otherwise unthinkable and threatening ideas.

The set of fantasies that are grouped together under the name of necrophilia signify something richer and altogether more complex than the joke would allow. Necrophilia hints at the imaginative collusion between life and death, an ambitious leap between the physical and the metaphysical. The obscure spark of desire in necrophilia lies precisely in the gap between the living erotic imagination and the object that is beyond desire. Fantasy operates by bridging the gap that is the threshold between the subject and the object of desire. In attempting to cross the threshold separating life from death, the ambition subtending necrophilia makes it one of the richest, liveliest and certainly most paradoxical desire types to be found in the lexicon of human sexuality. This book is about necrophilia, but not in its narrow or literal senses.

The desire for the dead was constituted as a psychological typology in early works of sexology by Richard von Krafft-Ebing and his contemporaries, who treated it warily as an instance of pathological perversion. More recent works of sexual science have changed little in their treatment of the subject, merely relabelling it under the umbrella term of 'paraphilia' (the fashionable word for the perversions in the contemporary field of abnormal psychology). In psychoanalytic literature, several journal articles have been devoted to the incidence of necrophilic phantasy in clinical practice.[2] The post-Freudian psychoanalysts Ernest Jones and Erich Fromm have both treated the subject of necrophilia in full-length works.[3] In the medico-legal sphere, one English article and two French theses have been devoted to necrophilia, as well as a full-length French work on the different types of sexual deviance involving the dead.[4]

Necrophilia has appeared from time to time in popular publications, too. Sergeant Bertrand, a nineteenth-century French soldier prosecuted for acts of violence towards and violation of corpses, was the subject of a recent biography by Michel Dansel.[5] Bertrand, whose court case took place in 1849 before the term 'necrophilia' had entered the medico-legal lexicon, was tried for acts of 'vampirism' and 'erotomania'. This case proved pivotal in moving on debates in medical circles regarding the 'correct' classification of such offenders.[6] Similarly, in the annals of English true crime, the cases of necrophile mass murderers John Christie and Dennis Nilsen have been documented by, respectively, Ludovic Kennedy in 1971 and Brian Masters in 1985.[7]

One of the primary difficulties faced when attempting a discussion of necrophilia is the problem of definition. The *Oxford English Dictionary* offers, rather vaguely: 'Fascination with death and dead bodies; *esp.* sexual attraction to dead bodies', while the *Robert* proposes the following—somewhat presumptuous—definition: 'Perversion sexuelle dans laquelle, habituellement, l'orgasme est obtenu au contact physique de cadavres.'[8] These definitions adhere closely to the etymology of the word: *nekro-*, the Greek prefix meaning 'corpse', and *philia*, meaning 'love of'. However, the problem with these layman's definitions is that they limit necrophilia to a single physical act. This is perhaps not surprising, given that dictionaries have neither the space nor the task to explore the psychology, cultural implications or phenomenology of the concepts they define.

One would assume, however, that reference books in the field of psychology would offer more insights into this obscure corner of the human imagination. A 1975 encyclopedia of psychology offers the longest definition I could find in a work of this type: 'Sexual acts on or with the dead body of a person or parts of it: a very rare sexually deviant and pathological (in the clinical sense) behaviour. Occurs in women as well as men.'[9] The *Oxford Dictionary of Psychology*, published as recently as 2001, differs very little except in terminology, and is not much more illuminating. It proposes: 'A paraphilia characterised by recurrent sexually arousing fantasies, sexual urges or behaviour involving intercourse with dead bodies.'[10] Dennis Nilsen, regarded by all published commentators as a necrophilic killer,[11] never performed sexual intercourse on the corpses he created. Similarly, Sergeant Bertrand stated in his testimony that he experienced more pleasure digging up and destroying corpses than violating them. Commentators on necrophilia, then, tend to focus somewhat erroneously on what the necrophile does, and are obsessed with the act that appears most obvious—sexual intercourse with the corpse. This may tell us as much about the commentators as it does about the necrophile, and, despite the mention of female necrophilia in the 1975 dictionary entry, the repeated focus on penetration of the corpse implicitly relegates necrophilia to the realms of male perversion.

Reducing necrophilia to a single, highly taboo act serves to distance us from its complexities. By maintaining focus on the alien nature of the behaviour, we do not have to consider the extent to which the necrophile's desires and unconscious fantasies may resemble yours or mine, and may have wider cultural implications. One of the best ways of maintaining a prohibition is to make the prohibited phenomenon remain radically other.

Brian Masters, the former French literary scholar who has become a renowned expert on serial killers, tries to take the definition of necrophilia further in his well-researched and thoughtful biography of Dennis Nilsen. He uses as his case material Nilsen's writings and confessions, as well as the case histories of other serial killers and a selection of imaginative literature on the subject. He concludes that the phenomenon of necrophilia can be seen in a person's overwhelming love of, or attraction to, death and destruction per se. He writes: 'A necrophiliac is not *only* a man who violates a corpse sexually (as popular belief holds), but a man for whom death is the ultimate beauty.'[12] The idealized, almost reverential tone hinted at by the suggestion of 'ultimate beauty' is perhaps not an exaggeration. In this book, I shall examine literary production which focuses on an aesthetic as well as sexual fascination with death and the dead. It can be argued that necrophilia is as much an aesthetic, a mode of representation, as it is a sexual perversion.

Throughout the history of sexological writing, commentators have disagreed on the exact nature of the necrophile's love object. While, for some, the corpse as a radically inanimate and passive object is central to an understanding of this perversion type, according to other thinkers it is the proximity to the idea of death and destruction that carries aphrodisiac properties. The much rarer term 'thanatophilia' also exists to describe an abstract (and usually de-sexualized) love of, or obsession with, death. However, for certain writers, 'necrophilia' encompasses the whole gamut of these variations.

In *The Anatomy of Human Destructiveness* (1974), Erich Fromm adopts and develops Hentig's character-based view of necrophilia.[13] Here, Fromm suggests a conflict within the human being between biophilous and necrophilous tendencies, where biophilia is a 'biologically normal impulse',[14] while necrophilia is a type of—by no means rare—pathology. According to Fromm, the necrophilous character is revealed in the following symptoms: '*the passionate attraction to all that is dead, decayed, putrid, sickly; it is the passion to transform that which is alive into something which is unalive; to destroy for the sake of destruction [...] It is the passion to "tear apart living structures"*'.[15] Fromm broadens considerably the scope of what can be understood by necrophilia. It becomes a descriptive model for the way in which desire operates in the human being, as significant as the biological reproductive imperative. Fromm's binary formulation biophilia/necrophilia is indebted to Freud's later model of the drives that establishes life instinct and death instinct as metapsychological principles. Despite the strong focus on sexual perversion and death in different parts of Freud's corpus, the literal meeting point of the two—*Triebmischung*—touches the conscious surface of Freud's work only occasionally. In the overt description and analysis of the perversions and their psychogenesis in 1905, sexual attraction to the dead merits a brief mention. In later works, Freud will go on to formulate full and complex theories of fetishism, sadism and masochism, which establish them as widespread cultural fantasies as well as local perversions, but no similar essay will be devoted to necrophilia.

From this brief presentation of existing wisdom, we can see that it is difficult to establish a consensus regarding the necrophile's identity, motivation, object or nature. Generalizations, presumptions and prejudices cloud the area of inquiry. It is my contention that, owing to its highly taboo nature, the understanding of necrophilia has not progressed very far in the hundred and fifty years during which sexual behaviour has been the subject of 'scientific' study. One of the aims of this book, then, will be to expand our understanding of the term 'necrophilia' and to make it available for literary and cultural criticism. Concepts such as this one have considerable elasticity within psychological and psychoanalytical discourses, and offer themselves readily for re-evaluation and recuperation.

In the course of this book, I shall re-examine psychoanalytic formulations of desire and death and analyse examples of literary necrophilia in order to destabilize epistemological preconceptions surrounding this term. In my reading, necrophilia will not be limited to acts of sexual intercourse with a dead body, nor restricted to a particular sort of gender relation, but will be recast as a central feature of the human fantasy relationship with death. Necrophilia thus becomes explicable as a desirous and idealizing relation to death, manifest in actual perversion or in representation. I am aware that in opening up the meaning of this term, I risk blurring boundaries between necrophilia and neighbouring phenomena. One can imagine, for example, the difficulty of gauging where sadism or fetishism stops, and necrophilia starts. I would like to suggest that it may not be helpful or even possible to draw such clear boundaries when discussing the multi-layered and complex realm of the erotic imagination. In the interests of my argument, however, I shall stress the validity of describing an apparently sadistic depiction of sexual murder as necrophilic, if the focus is on creating and enjoying death rather than enjoyment in inflicting pain. The term will be a mutable one, as it will be used both to name the specific cultural fantasies in question, and to draw attention to its own cultural specificity, its status as a product of a historical moment.

Secondly, I am aware that my privileging of this term is itself potentially problematic. The careful taxonomy of sexual perversions (sadism, fetishism, necrophilia) is precisely the historical intellectual tradition that this study (and such illustrious precedents as Foucault's

Histoire de la sexualité, 1976) put under scrutiny and, to some extent, undermine. The value of reconsidering these terms is precisely to question our preconceptions about the ways in which the human imagination has been categorized and interpreted. The power of naming sexuality was wielded firstly by the church and secondly by the sexologists (and, according to Foucault, these institutions were equally conservative in their use of this power in the service of societal control of others). It is my intention to appropriate this power of naming for revisionist purposes. This book represents one modest attempt to put into question and open up for re-examination the commonplaces surrounding our perceptions of sexual desire.

On Sex and Death in Western Culture

If there is a scarcity of scientific and informative literature to be found on necrophilia, then rather the opposite is true in the case of imaginative, artistic and philosophical material. The assumption that sexual desire and death are intimately connected is deep-rooted and widely represented in our culture. This commonplace is illustrated by the French expression for 'orgasm'—*la petite mort*—which has been imported wholesale into most European languages, such is its affective resonance.

The notion of orgasmic pleasure coming through a deathly consummation has been a recurrent feature of the sexual imagination in art. It is prevalent in the classics (remember that Aphrodite, the goddess of love herself, sprang from the semen of a murdered man). It is reflected in the many representations of Tristan and Isolde's *Liebestod*, from the medieval texts to Wagner's Romantic musical hyperbole. And, as we enter the twenty-first century, it is with us as much as ever, in our contemporary cinematic obsession with sexual perversion culminating in ecstatic death.[16]

As post-Freudians, we may talk about art as facilitating a return of the cultural repressed, that is as a collective reminder of the most disturbing and exciting aspects of our humanness, aspects which consciously we overlook or reject. Such an understanding would explain why so much of Western art has taken as its subject matter those liminal states which fascinate us while threatening our sense of stability: sexuality, the ultimate unknowable concept that is death, and the complex web we spin between them.

Art shares with religion and philosophy the task of representing, encoding and giving sense to our fearful and problematic human relation to death. Anthropologists and social scientists examine the elaborate rituals created by so-called civilized and uncivilized societies alike to deal with the dead and to readjust the living to the sudden absence of a life. Each culture and historical epoch has designated an appropriate way of symbolizing the passage into death. These range from the water-filled limestone wells in which Maya communities housed the dead and their decorative relics, through the mysteries that are the Egyptian pyramids, to the English Victorian cult of mourning. The latter is emblematized at its most absurd and maudlin by jewellery made from a lock of hair of the dear departed or enamelled brooches and rings showing an abject woman wailing over a tomb.[17]

Such Western attempts to banalize and domesticate death by making it into a decorative conceit can be seen as a manifestation of the universal need to tame death, to make familiar what is radically other. The Victorian fashion for mourning and Pre-Raphaelite images of beautiful dead women create idealized representations removed from the frightening abyssal reality of decay and decomposition. John Everett Millais's representation of the dead Ophelia (1852) as a waxy, ethereal, doll-like figure is a perfect example of this highly aestheticized fetishization. It is an approach to something terrifying and inconceivable in the real, which is controlled by the safety mechanism of artistic discipline and convention. On the other hand, this attempt to bring death, through symbolization, into the art gallery and the home can reveal a paradoxical attraction to, or desire for, death. It can be seen as an attempt to represent in positive terms an absence, a void in comprehension. Thus, attraction and repulsion are balanced in a complex and delicate relation.

It is here that we may notice a similarity in technique in the cultural treatment of death and sexual desire. Both sexuality and death are represented by displacing or projecting the desire felt by the one onto the other. Feminists have pointed out that in the Western patriarchal tradition, otherness has conventionally been defined as femininity. The history of representations reveals multiple examples of how both sexuality and death, perceived as threats to the unity of the masculine subject, have been projected onto the figure of the woman. Starting with Lilith and Eve, women have been associated with a sexual temptation that carries the threat of the fall, the annihilation of male power. Male representations of women have sexualized them using a rhetoric of metonymic displacement. Blamed for exciting men, the female body has been made into the locus of that desire, the carrier of potential male annihilation. Like death itself, women have been feared and desired.

While one side of the coin of this fearful misogyny produces representations of woman as the deathly seducer, the other side is characterized by the figure of woman as dead body. Representations of beautiful female corpses allow male artists to maintain death in the field of alterity: it is visited on the guilty other, while the attraction of death may be displaced and contained within the image of beautiful passive womanhood.[18] Graves's poem 'Penthesileia' recounts Achilles' necrophilic excesses on the dead body of the warrior queen:

> Penthesileia, dead of profuse wounds,
> Was despoiled of her arms by Prince Achilles,
> Who, for love of that fierce white naked corpse,
> Necrophily on her committed
> In the public view.[19]

In this poem, a woman who has excited by her appetite and capacity for killing is finally enjoyed in her own death. In 'despoiling her of her arms', Achilles completes the process of feminization which death has begun.

The femme fatale in art, then, both gives death in return for male sexual weakness and receives death as the punishment for her wantonness. This aspect of patriarchy's artistic practice is the subject of a full-length study by Elisabeth Bronfen, *Over her Dead Body* (1992). In this book, she reads representations of dead women as social symptoms, that is, as the failed repression of cultural obsessions which are then relocated in a symbol: 'representations are symptoms that visualise even as they conceal what is too dangerous to articulate openly but too fascinating to repress successfully. They repress by localising death away from the self, at the body of a beautiful woman, at the same time that this representation lets the repressed return, albeit in a disguised manner.'[20] According to Bronfen, death, sexuality and otherness are almost always located in the female signifying body. It is thus that they are simultaneously kept at bay and vicariously enjoyed.

Bronfen's work provides a convincing argument to account for the prevalence of this artistic feature in the early-modern period to the present. As the myth of Pygmalion would suggest, artistic production and life-giving have been traditionally linked. Several feminists have deconstructed the widespread prejudice that creative energy is essentially masculine. This is exposed as a jealous male fantasy designed to compensate for lack of the female capacity to give birth. Hence, works of art are seen to spring from the male cerebrum just as Athena sprang from Pallas's head. Christine Battersby's *Gender and Genius* undertakes a particularly thorough and searing deconstruction of male history's 'seminal' works and the jealous refusal on the part of the male to attribute cerebral creative strength to women.[21]

However, while very much admiring such feminist critiques, I would also inject a note of caution. When considering necrophilic representations, it is important to keep in sight the fact that some representations of beautiful male corpses also exist (one thinks immediately of Henry Wallis's *Death of Chatterton*, 1856), suggesting at least a subculture of homoerotic necrophilic representations. Moreover, we may notice that with increasing female participation in the artistic and literary sphere, various erotic explorations of death and fetishization of corpses, both male and female, have been undertaken by female artists. The question must be asked: is there something innately 'masculine' about the privileging of the image of the dead other? Or does the fact that, owing to numerous socio-economic and cultural factors, there have always been more male artists than female ones account for the fact that there are more representations by men of dead women than by women of dead men? If mid-nineteenth-century society had allowed for a female Edgar Poe, how can we know that she would not have written that the death of a beautiful man is, unquestionably, the most poetical topic in the world?[22]

The Italian feminist philosopher Adriana Cavarero has suggested that the tendency to understand subjectivity in relation to mortality is a feature of a masculine philosophical tradition.[23] Developing work done by Luce Irigaray, she argues for a feminine consciousness of 'natality' as an imaginary and spatial alternative to the finitude-driven and temporal masculine economy. While I can appreciate the polemical gesture that Caverero is making by showing up the gender bias of Western philosophy, it strikes me that this is only a partial answer. The perception that death is intrinsically masculine risks eradicating the possibility of either a feminine or properly universal relation to tension, time, change and decay, all of which constitute human life. Both men and women can—and will—die. It is important to separate this neutral biological and psychological reality from the dominant cultural fantasies of death and the discourses which are constructed around it. Replacing mortality with natality does not address the ongoing need for a set of tools with which to explore our relationship to our finitude. The extent to which the genders experience and artistically represent their fear and desire for death differently within existing philosophical frameworks will be one of the questions I bear in mind throughout this study.

Critical Perceptions of the French Nineteenth Century

Although they have made frequent appearances throughout the history of representation, the death-desire couple and the necrophilic body have inhabited different guises and received diverse treatments according to the tastes and the conventions of a given epoch or country. While it is important to bear in mind the vast history and geography associated with these ideas, and the extent to which they are an important constitutive part of our collective psyche, it may be most profitable to examine local examples of these phenomena in close detail. The course of the nineteenth century in France is one such period at which there is evidence of a concentration of artistic interest in portraying the dead or dying body and in exploring the relation between fear and desire with regard to death and sexuality. The second half of the century provides a particularly rich localized nexus of such representations.

The nineteenth century in France, as elsewhere in Europe, has traditionally been seen as an epoch of great social and scientific progress, optimism and growth. It saw the second wave of colonialization, the celebration of French engineering in the great exhibitions, and a general spirit of *élan vital*. It is therefore to be expected that French literature of the period will contain evidence of this flourishing society and will echo its optimistic spirit. Balzac's conception of the *comédie humaine*, which attempts to describe and analyse all of human life, and Zola's pseudo-scientific school of Naturalism are just two examples of the literary imagination embodying the same scope and breadth as contemporary socio-economic projects.

Yet there is a different and quite contrary face of the nineteenth-century imagination in France, one which is overlooked if we concentrate only on the larger picture of social expansion. In the political sphere, this is characterized by repeated periods of civil unrest and governmental instability and change, giving rise to an atmosphere of discontent and division. On the socio-economic level, the mortality rate was high for much of the century and several epidemics raged through newly industrial France, breeding and killing in the claustrophobic intensity of crowded tenement buildings. Several artistic innovations of the period are similarly characterized by an insidious morbidity which may be seen to reveal the underside of the century's visible optimism. In the literary sphere, waning Romanticism spawns the delirious Gothic hyperbole of the Frenetic Romantics. Classical music adopts a mortuary aesthetic with such works as Berlioz's *Symphonie fantastique* (1830). Meanwhile, pictorial art focuses on death-haunted subjects, including the battle scenes of Géricault and the epic-scale murder and sadism of Delacroix.

Moreover, where there are signs of decay and death, there are frequently signs of aestheticized eroticism and pleasure. Deathbed scenes become favoured loci of libidinal expression, as in *Madame Bovary*, where Emma's horrible death is dwelt on with loving attention and sensuous appeal, and Zola's *Nana*, where the eponymous heroine embodies an excessive sexuality which is seen to lead inexorably to her own dramatic demise. The deathbed is traditionally a place heavy with religious associations, and indeed in *Madame Bovary*, Flaubert has the adulterous and hypocritically pious Emma take ostentatious pains to receive her last rites. In these passages of the book, religious and erotic descriptions of her body and soul are found occupying the same space.

This blasphemous blending of the religious and the erotic in the description of the dying or dead body can be read in the general context of the changing status of religious belief at the time. Such writers as Flaubert, Baudelaire and Villiers de l'Isle-Adam describe the sacrilegious debasement of sacred objects, while promoting fetishized sexual objects to the status of the divine.[24] This technique points towards a change in consciousness that takes place in the century, whereby the prescriptions and proscriptions of Christianity with regard to sexual desire and behaviour begin to be challenged.

The powerful province of the church in medieval times becomes the province of medicine in modernity. Charcot and others brought desire and disease into the public eye, encapsulated in the *maladie du siècle*, hysteria. The ostentatious exhibitions of women's bodies crippled with hysterical symptoms is a central image of the nineteenth century, suggesting a fashion for, and interest in, the sick body. Art sought to respond to this trend in science with the well-known painting of the *Leçon de Charcot à la Salpêtrière* (1887) by Pierre-André Brouillet.

This perverse aspect of the century's literary imagination was first taken into account by Mario Praz in *The Romantic Agony* (1933). This work treats the nineteenth century in Europe as characterized by a taste for destructive sexual excess and reads literature through the lens of the perverse sexual imagination. In this it is rare, as earlier—and even subsequent—critical studies have tended rather to sanitize literary production and refuse the possibility of reading images of sexual perversion at the literal level. Structuralism gave an excuse to those critics with a taste for avoiding the close details of a work of art's imaginative content, and thereby removed a whole series of layers of understanding and appreciation, relegating reading practice to the bare bones of prosody and form.

In nineteenth-century French literature, there is a wealth of representations of death and decay tinged with morbid delectation, such that when trying to establish which texts one might include in a 'nineteenth-century French necrophilic canon', one is rather spoilt for choice.

The influence of writers of fantastic morbid literature like Jacques Cazotte (1719–92) and Charles Nodier (1780–1844) is strongly felt in the early nineteenth century. Coming out of this tradition, Jules Janin (1804–74) mixes terror, humour and cynicism in such works as *L'Âne mort et la femme guillotinée* (1829), which presents an early example of morbid eroticism in the horror mode.

The strain of literature known as Frenetic Romanticism, popular in the 1830s, carries on this tradition. Necrophilia is a staple ingredient of these works, and a particularly suitable candidate for the canon is Pétrus Borel (1809–59). Borel's *Champavert: contes immoraux* (1833) includes elements of murder and dissection, recounted in a hyperbolic Gothic prose style. Prosper Mérimée (1803–70) is another significant figure. His *conte* 'La Vénus d'Ille' (1837) recounts the tale of a bronze statue of a woman which comes to life and suffocates to death in its embrace an unwitting young man. The most famous of the Frenetic Romantics is Théophile Gautier (1811–72), whose *contes fantastiques* are structured around narratives of slippage between life and death, desire and mortality. Gautier's later poetic work *Émaux et camées* (1852) exemplifies the cold austerity of Parnassian anti-utilitarianism. However, it still calls upon motifs familiar to the Gothic imagination of his earlier writing, such as the mummified hand of a murderer in 'Lacenaire' and the erotic dance of death in 'Poëme de la femme'.

Later in the century, Baudelaire's translations of Poe's short stories brought mainstream 'high-cultural' morbid prose to the French reading public. Mallarmé's translation of such poems as 'The Raven', in 1875, did the same for poetry. Also in the poetic line, Lautréamont's *Chants de Maldoror* (1868–9) immediately suggests itself as a relevant excursion into destructive eroticism. The poem's depiction of a homicidal prowler and his dead male victims could provide insight into a strain of the necrophilic imagination. *Les Névroses* (1883) by the little-known Symbolist poet Maurice Rollinat (1846–1903) also contains many images reminiscent of the 'mortuary aesthetic', most notably the poem entitled 'La Putréfaction'.

The *fin-de-siècle* taste for Decadence is another rich source of necrophilic imagery. *Contes cruels* of 1883 by Villiers de L'Isle-Adam (1838–89) contains 'Véra', a tale of a dead beloved, remniscent of Poe's 'Ligeia' and 'Morella'. It tells of a husband's desire to have his wife alive again, and the counter-desire to unite with her dead body, which is presented as a forbidden and unspoken fetish object. Also, *L'Ève future* (1886) is an experiment in science-fiction writing in which the figure of a female automaton provides a lifeless object of sexual desire—perhaps the first example of cyber-necrophilia.

It will be noted that the majority of these writers are male. However, a contribution to necrophilic writing by women is a short story by Isabelle Eberhardt (1877–1904), 'Infernalia: volupté sépulcrale'. Georges Rodenbach (1855–98) is responsible for Belgium's best-known contribution to francophone necrophilic literature, with *Bruges-la-morte* (1892). This novel unites the Poësque theme of sexual love for a dead wife with a desolate depiction of the city of Bruges. Because of the heavy insistence on loss, mourning and a deathly aesthetic, Bachelard has described the novel as an illustration of the 'Ophelia complex'.

While there are many nineteenth-century French works which would serve to illustrate the necrophilic literary imagination, I shall limit my close readings in this book to texts by two authors which I have not yet discussed. They are *Les Fleurs du Mal* and selected prose by Charles Baudelaire (1821–67), and *Monsieur Vénus, La Tour d'amour* and *Le Grand Saigneur* by Rachilde (Marguerite Eymery Vallette) (1860–1953).

The case of Baudelaire requires particular attention, as his artistic and philosophical sensibility has become synonymous with the mid-century in French literature, but no study exists which looks uniquely at Baudelaire's poetics through the lens of his destructive erotic themes and treatments. I shall argue that the tendency to read the poet's fascination with the erotic and mortality separately rather than as facets of the same fantasy is a serious lacuna in Baudelaire studies. Rachilde represents the *fin-de-siècle* Decadent aesthetic, and also she represents the desirous voice of the female artist who has struggled to be heard throughout the century. Yet, unlike most recent studies of Rachilde, my inquiry will not focus on her texts principally as examples of women's writing, explicitly treating of questions of female subjectivity, but as paradigms of deathly desire which effectively suspend and disrupt our understanding of gender.

My harnessing and juxtaposing of a major writer of the Western canon and an—until recently—little-known female Decadent writer is not accidental. Beyond their particular places within a given literary school or tradition, the works of these writers are linked primarily by their privileging of certain repetitive tropes, images and ideas surrounding desire. The motif of the dead body and the descriptions of murderous sexuality within the works indicate a common preoccupation and, I shall argue, reveal a principal level of signification. Moreover, the writers gesture, by means of shared cultural references and intertextual allusions, to a wider sub-canon of names associated with death and desire. These incorporate both earlier and contemporary writers with similar preoccupations, such as the Marquis de Sade and Gautier, and figures of legend, history and myth, such as the vampire.

This book, then, is not a survey of the whole of nineteenth-century French necrophilia, even though the wealth of available material in France, as evidenced by Praz's study and by the brief inventory of names and titles I have just given, would make this possible. Rather, the book will look closely at the way in which two key authors' texts work as literary and imaginative models, elucidating the cultural fantasy of necrophilia.

Methods, Texts and Tools

Much has been written on the problematic and seductive coupling of psychoanalytic and literary theory. This book will add to the body of work which deals with these theoretical questions, as it will take this relation as a central one in the attempt to understand and theorize the concept which forms the subject of my inquiries. Psychoanalysis will play two roles in this study. Firstly, it will be viewed as a historically relevant theoretical discourse, which sets out to analyse similar questions of human desire to those posed in the literary texts. Freudian psychoanalytic works will be discussed and their rhetoric analysed as texts in their own right. Secondly, the paradigms of desire offered by psychoanalysis will be evaluated for their ability to describe and account for the concept under study. In the last few years, academic writing on death in literature and art has tended to come, not so much from literary or even psychoanalytic scholars, as from the emergent field of social science known as death studies. This interdisciplinary field, spanning philosophy, the arts, history, geography and economics, takes the human relation to death as its key epistemological framework.[25] The current book is similarly hybrid in its scope, borrowing from and contributing to the fields of literary studies, psychoanalytic criticism and the history of ideas. Because of this, my interdisciplinary reconceptualization of necrophilia may be properly described as addressing the concerns of the field of death studies.

This book will start with history, progress through theory and accord the last word to literature. Chapter 1 will trace the history of thinking and writing about necrophilia in the French nineteenth century. In Chapter 2, which deals with Freudian psychoanalytic theory, I shall examine the usefulness of the concept of the death drive for a re-evaluation of necrophilia. Chapters 4 and 5 will take the form of literary case studies, drawn from the writing of Baudelaire and Rachilde, which will analyse literary means by which the mechanisms described by Freud are articulated. I shall conclude by evaluating the inheritance of these nineteenth-century preoccupations in the cultural imaginary of subsequent centuries.

Notes to the Introduction

1. Cited in preface to Gabrielle Wittkop, *Le Nécrophile*, and F. de Gaudenzi, *Nécropolis* (Paris: La Musardine, 1998), 5.
2. See Hannah Segal, 'A necrophilic phantasy', *International Journal of Psychoanalysis* 34 (1953), 90–104; Victor Calef and Edward M. Weinshel, 'Certain neurotic equivalents of necrophilia', *International Journal of Psychoanalysis* 53 (1972), 67–76; Joseph S. Bierman, 'Necrophilia in a thirteen-year-old boy', *Psychoanalytic Quarterly* 31 (1962), 329–36.
3. Ernest Jones, *On the Nightmare* (London: The Hogarth Press and the Institute of Psycho-Analysis, 1931); Erich Fromm, *The Anatomy of Human Destructiveness* (London: Jonathan Cape, 1974).
4. See A. Bartholomew, K. Milte and F. Galbally, 'Homosexual necrophilia', *Medicine, Science and the Law* 18/1 (1978), 29–35; Pierre Bonvalet, 'De la violation

de sépultures', doctoral thesis (Marseilles, 1956); Pierre Desrosières, 'À propos d'un cas de nécrophilie', doctoral thesis (Créteil, 1974), and Alexis Épaulard, *Nécrophilie, nécrosadisme, nécrophagie* (Lyons: A. Storck, 1901).

5. Michel Dansel, *Le Sergent Bertrand: portrait d'un nécrophile heureux* (Paris: Albin Michel, 1991).

6. See Vernon A. Rosario, *The Erotic Imagination: French Histories of Perversity* (Oxford: Oxford University Press, 1997), 58–67.

7. Ludovic Kennedy, *10, Rillington Place* (London: Panther, 1971), and Brian Masters, *Killing for Company: The Case of Dennis Nilsen* (London: Jonathan Cape, 1985).

8. One cannot help but wonder how the writer of this entry would know how (or even whether) a necrophile obtains orgasm in the pursuit of his or her pleasure.

9. *Encyclopaedia of Psychology*, 2 vols., ed. H. J. Eysenck, W. J. Arnold and R. Meili (Suffolk: Fontana, 1975), ii. 705.

10. Andrew M. Coleman, *Dictionary of Psychology* (Oxford: Oxford University Press, 2001), 479.

11. As well as Brian Masters's biography, several writers in the field of cultural studies have used Nilsen's case to discuss the sociological implications of murder. Among them are Deborah Cameron and Elizabeth Frazer in *The Lust to Kill* (Cambridge: Polity, 1987) and Josephine McDonagh in 'Do or die: problems of agency and gender in the aesthetics of murder', *Genders* 5 (summer 1989), 120–34. Interest in Nilsen can be explained partly by the killer's prolific attempts at self-definition and representation of his imaginative world and acts, in a series of poems, drawings and a prison journal.

12. Masters, *Killing for Company*, 278.

13. e.g. Hans von Hentig, *Der Nekrotope Mensch* (Stuttgart: F. Enke, 1964).

14. Erich Fromm, *The Anatomy of Human Destructiveness* (London: Jonathan Cape, 1974), 366.

15. Ibid., 332 (Fromm's italics).

16. Two of the most extreme and explicit examples of this conceit in art-house film-making are Nagisa Oshima's *Ai no corrida* (*In the Realm of the Senses*) (Japan, 1976), now a cult film in Western Europe, and Almodóvar's *Matador* (Spain, 1985). In both of these films, killing or being killed at the moment of orgasm represents the ultimate sexual pleasure. The films of Hitchcock and Buñuel are also rich sites of the sex-death obsession.

17. A good selection of mourning jewellery can be seen in the jewellery room of the Victoria and Albert Museum, London.

18. See Bram Dijkstra, *Idols of Perversity: Fantasies of Feminine Evil in Fin-de-Siècle Culture* (Oxford: Oxford University Press, 1986). The thesis of this book is that at the end of the nineteenth century, sick and dying women were promoted as idols of virtuous femininity. This is interpreted as a tactic to ensure the continued social oppression of women.

19. Robert Graves, *Complete Poems*, ed. Beryl Graves and Dunstan Ward, 2 vols. (Manchester: Carcanet, 1997), i. 221.

20. Elisabeth Bronfen, *Over her Dead Body: Death, Femininity and the Aesthetic* (Manchester: Manchester University Press, 1992), p. xi.

21. Christine Battersby, *Gender and Genius: Towards a Feminist Aesthetics* (London: The Women's Press, 1989).

22. My reading of Rachilde's novels in Chapter 4 will attempt to answer this question. It is not inconceivable that Rachilde, who is perhaps the nearest thing we have to a French female Poe, would have agreed with this statement. Poe's famous dictum is found in 'The philosophy of composition', in *Essays and Reviews* (New York: Literary Classics of the United States, 1984), 19.

23. Adriana Cavarero, *In Spite of Plato: A Feminist Rewriting of Ancient Philosophy*, trans. Serena Anderlini-D'Onofrio and Aine O'Healy (Cambridge: Polity, 1995).

24. For a more detailed discussion of this idea, see my article 'Ecstasies and agonies: the "oceanic feeling", God and sexuality in Baudelaire and Villiers de l'Isle-Adam', in *(Un)Faithful Texts: Religion in French and Francophone Literature from the 1780s to the 1980s*, ed. Paul Cooke and Jane Lee (New Orleans: University Press of the South, 2000), 53–66.

25. Recent examples of works of death studies that touch on literary questions are *Death and Representation*, ed. Sarah Webster Goodwin and Elisabeth Bronfen (Baltimore: Johns Hopkins University Press, 1993); *The Limits of Death: Between Philosophy and Psychoanalysis*, ed. Joanne Morra, Mark Robson and Marquand Smith (Manchester: Manchester University Press, 2000), and Jonathan Dollimore's ambitious tome detailing the close alliance of Eros and Thanatos throughout the history of Western literature and philosophy: *Death, Desire and Loss in Western Culture* (London: Allen Lane, Penguin, 1998).

CHAPTER 1

From Sade to Sexology

Il n'y a que du désir et du social et rien d'autre.

GILLES DELEUZE and FÉLIX GUATTARI[1]

In the Introduction, I briefly detailed some of the sources of opinion, theory and information about necrophilia available to the reader. These included social and medical discursive texts, produced within such disciplines as sexology and psychoanalysis, written confessions and journals by necrophiles and murderers, and, of course, literature and art. In this chapter, I shall attempt to chart the history of such thinking about perverse sexuality, particularly necrophilia, by excavating its roots in the nineteenth century. This will be done by means of a textual examination of the major intertexts, influences and relationships between theoretical discourses and literary production.

To examine the attitudes to dead bodies and the presence of necrophilia in a given epoch, one could look in a variety of places. Police reports, court documents and newspaper accounts all suggest themselves as relevant sources of historical data. A historian could doubtless produce a convincing picture of the populace's relationship to death and violence in a given epoch by working closely with such archival material.[2] However, in the interests of concision and tractability, I shall limit my reading of non-literary texts to a small corpus of external sources. Bearing in mind the literariness of my focus and the close-textual nature of my approach, I shall draw only on such sources as are relevant to my key corpus of texts in a variety of ways, which I shall sketch out below.

Firstly, where the key literary texts allude to or may be influenced by other textual production, for example in investigating the nineteenth-century reception of the Marquis de Sade, I shall undertake readings of contemporary comments, opinions and references to this writer in literary journals, memoirs and other publications. Secondly, where the key literary texts are themselves the subject of discursive textual production, as in the writings of the degeneration theorists, a deconstructive reading of the rhetoric of the theory will be undertaken.

Finally, where discursive textual production may be seen to be treating the same concerns as the key literary texts, such as German sexological accounts which present case studies of necrophilia as evidential material for understanding human desire, a brief comparative reading of rhetorical and textual devices will be attempted.

The Marquis de Sade: a Legendary Forebear

Any study of sexual perversion in literature would be incomplete without a discussion of the Marquis de Sade's influence in shaping cultural and aesthetic attitudes towards prohibited or transgressive desires. Sade's name is synonymous with extreme perversion, and indeed, throughout the history of Western thought, no individual has been more encyclopedic in her or his coverage of the possibilities open to the sexual imagination. In acknowledgement of this fact, various critical studies of the nineteenth century and of its individual authors have already treated the question of Sade as a perverse paternal literary figure.[3]

Rather than tracing echoes of Sade in subsequent texts, I shall briefly attempt below to ascertain the status of Sade's reputation for nineteenth-century writers. I will do this firstly by establishing the availability of the texts during the century as readily acquired or clandestine commodities, and secondly by looking at the legendary or mythical status of the persona of Sade in the nineteenth century, and attempt to see what it signified.

Donatien-Alphonse-François de Sade (1740–1814) is doubtless one of the first writers to include necrophilia as a type of sexual behaviour in his libertine writing.[4] Libertinage, which in Diderot and D'Alembert's *Encyclopédie* is defined simply as 'l'habitude de céder à l'instinct qui nous porte aux plaisirs des sens',[5] takes on a new dimension in *Les Cent-vingt Journées de Sodome* (written 1785, first published 1904), *Justine, ou les Malheurs de la vertu* (1791) and *Juliette* (1797). In these texts, the essence of libertinage is destruction and murder, and the desecrated bodies of victims litter the corpus.

In *Les Cent-vingt Journées de Sodome*, the exhaustive catalogue of sexual pleasures runs from fairly mild flagellation, through coprophagic excesses and simulated necrophilia (live girls dressed as corpses and laid out in coffins for the libertines' pleasure), to eventual torture, murder and literal necrophilia. The form of Sade's unfinished work is that of dialogue within dialogue, so that these themes are first introduced and illustrated by the quartet of prostitutes whose job it is to entertain the four reclusive libertines, after which the dramatis personae will play out versions of the described perversion types.

For example, Duclos, the prostitute, recounts the following anecdote of a necrophilic client:

Vous savez que l'usage, à Paris, est d'exposer les morts aux portes des maisons. Il y avait un homme dans le monde qui me payait douze francs par chacun de ces appareils lugubres où je pouvais le conduire dans ma soirée. Toute sa volupté consistait à s'en approcher avec moi le plus près possible, au bord même du cercueil, si nous pouvions, et là, je devais le branler en sorte que son foutre éjaculât sur le cercueil. Nous en allions courir comme cela trois ou quatre dans la soirée.[6]

This mild case, in which the libertine described is content merely to masturbate in close proximity to death, serves as anecdotal erotic fuel to the listeners in the story and to the text's readers. In the final section of the text, Sade describes 150 'passions meurtrières', in which elements of sadism and necrophilia mix and the aim is the annihilation of a victim in a manner causing a particular aesthetic and sexual thrill for the protagonist. The following is a typical example: 'Un grand partisan de culs étrangle une mère en l'enculant; quand elle est morte, il la retourne et la fout en con. En déchargeant, il tue la fille sur le sein de la mère à coup de couteau dans le sein, puis il fout la fille en cul quoique morte [...].'[7] While there is relatively little description of intercourse with corpses in Sade, there is certainly ample evidence of the celebration and derivation of sexual pleasure from the contemplation or achievement of destruction. Inflicting death presents the ultimate passage to sensuous pleasure, and contemplation of the corpse represents both an aesthetic and an erotic celebration. Necrophilia, or the breaking down of boundaries between life and death in the service of erotic stimulation, maps perfectly onto Sade's aesthetic innovations, such as the mixing of high and low registers and the collapse of linear narrative in the enumerative profusion of perversion types.

Sade's view of exaltation in destruction draws on the notion that nothing is unnatural as, in order for an action to be able to take place,

Nature must already allow for it within her system. The transgressive pleasure comes, however, in opposing the falsely constructed social laws which are seen to be wholly in opposition to Nature's intentions. The encoding of what is 'natural' in culture causes a schism between chaos and ordered revolt or anarchy. Sade's fantasies are violent attacks on the state and on the individual body, both of which must be forcibly reduced to their essence—death.

It is not until the twentieth century that Sade is routinely and explicitly acknowledged by other writers and is elevated to canonical respectability by the scholarly literary critic.[8] Nonetheless, Sade's influence on the nineteenth-century literary imagination is attested by Sainte-Beuve in 1843:

J'oserai affirmer, sans crainte d'être démenti, que Byron et de Sade (je demande pardon au rapprochement) ont peut-être été les deux plus grands inspirateurs de nos modernes, l'un affiché et visible, l'autre clandestin—pas trop clandestin. En lisant certains de nos romanciers en vogue, si vous voulez le fond du coffre, l'escalier secret de l'alcôve, ne perdez jamais cette dernière clé.[9]

Sainte-Beuve situates Sade at the heart of the modernist imagination and in an interesting relation of semi-secrecy. Sade's contribution is 'clandestin—pas trop clandestin'. This raises the question of quite how well known and how widely read Sade's texts themselves actually were for the nineteenth-century literary population, and to what extent his massive reputation rests on rumour, legend and hearsay.

Following the Revolution, the reprinting of Sade's texts was banned. That decision, taken in 1814, was upheld in French courts until as recently as 1957.[10] However, this in no way suggests that editions of Sade were not in circulation during the period of restriction, but these often appear to have been in incomplete or fragmented form. In 1839, Flaubert experienced some difficulty in getting hold of a copy, as his correspondence tells us: 'Ô mon cher Ernest, à propos du marquis de Sade, si tu pouvais me trouver quelques-uns des romans de cet honnête écrivain, je te les payerais leur pesant d'or.'[11] Apparently his search was successful, as he writes in 1841: 'Quand on a lu le marquis de Sade et qu'on est revenu de l'éblouissement, on se prend à se demander si tout ne serait pas vrai, si la verité n'était pas tout ce qu'il enseigne'.[12] For Flaubert at least, then, a reading of Sade is not disappointing and has tremendous emotional and rhetorical power, causing *l'éblouissement* and laying claim to the 'truth'.

Flaubert's fascination with Sade is well documented in the Goncourts' literary journal ('c'est étonnant, ce de Sade, on le trouve à tous les bouts de Flaubert comme un horizon'[13]). Indeed, frequent mention is made of Sade in various contexts in this great conspectus on the literary tastes of the time. (I counted thirty-eight appearances of his name.) This suggests that during the nineteenth century, Sade's name is incorporated into the canon of great writers, but that it lurks on the margins, as a byword for extremity and taboo, thereby attracting to it the glamour of forbidden authority.

It is not clear just how widely read Sade was in the early part of the century, and there is reason to be suspicious of many writers' claims that they had read his work at first hand.[14] By 1850, however, it was certainly possible for Jules Michelet to read *Justine* in the library: 'j'allai prendre à la bibliothèque ce livre atroce du marquis de Sade et je le vomis le lendemain'.[15] The strong and visceral language of disapproval found in Michelet's statement suggests that the stigma of dangerous immorality which post-revolutionary fervour accorded to Sade is maintained by the conservative fringe of nineteenth-century thinkers.

Sade's name is known and used by writers of the century, usually to evoke a certain image of political and sexual subjecthood, an archetype of transgression. Borel's *Mme Putiphar* (1839) salutes Sade's work as a glorious anti-heroic textual corpus, which he evidently expects to be only too recognizable to his readers: 'Cette gloire de la France, [...] l'illustre auteur d'un livre contre lequel vous criez tous à l'infamie et que vous avez tous dans votre poche, [...] très haut et très puissant seigneur, monsieur le comte de Sade.'[16] The double-edged nature of Sade's infamy and fame is brought to the reader's attention again. Sainte-Beuve's 'clandestin — pas trop clandestin' is echoed in the idea of the hypocritical relationship between Sade's texts and the reading public. He represents that which is publicly decried and privately, pruriently enjoyed. Both in the illicit procuring of these condemned texts for readerly enjoyment, as in the case of Flaubert, and in the suggested hypocrisy here within the *bien-pensant*'s relation to Sade, we see that he functioned as a kind of high-cultural repressed, a literary taboo, for the nineteenth century.

From these examples, as from many others that I could cite here, it becomes apparent that the proper name of Sade comes to stand metonymically for a certain group of associated ideas. The texts themselves take on the status of forbidden objects of desire, while the adjective 'sadique' enters writerly currency, decades before 'sadisme' is coined to describe the sexual perversion. This is seen in the following extract from the Goncourts' *Journal*: 'Henkey, l'anglais sadique, contait dans sa loge au bal de l'opéra à Saint-Victor, comme un beau trait, qu'un amant d'Emma Vali, prêt à crever, lui fit promettre, comme désir suprême de venir pisser sur sa tombe.'[17] More generally, 'sadique' becomes the convenient byword for a certain artistic taste characteristic of the nineteenth-century penchant for cruelty and excess. For example, Jules Lemaître speaks of 'le mysticisme sadique de M Barbey D'Aurevilly' to express that writer's often tortured and cruel poetic vision.[18]

The ambiguous status of the Sadeian text as explored above is similar to the mythical status that the figure of Sade the man acquires during the period. In 1835, the actor Fleury writes of Sade in his memoirs: 'homme puissant, seigneur renommé, haute intelligence obscurcie par le crime, membre d'une race illustre entre toutes celles de la France'.[19] Fleury also wants to draw rhetorical attention to Sade's greatness. He foregrounds Sade's renown as a figure associated dually with aristocracy and crime, positing a tacit link between the two, suggesting the figure of the gentleman criminal who was a popular figure for the Romantics and for writers like Balzac.

Notice also Flaubert's formulation 'j'aime bien à voir des hommes comme ça, comme Néron, comme le marquis de Sade'.[20] Here, Sade becomes a monster of equivalent stature to the monsters of history and the classics. It is a considerable triumph for his posthumous career as a figure of brutality and infamy that only twenty-five years after his death he has achieved parity with Nero for a writer like Flaubert.

This popular association of Sade as a criminal demon, which is glorified and romanticized in the nineteenth century, began with popular rumours and eighteenth-century press accounts of Sade's acts of sexual impropriety and brutality towards prostitutes, most notably the Rose Keller scandal in 1768.[21] *Faits divers* would make a legend of Sade, often exaggerating the extent of his acts of brutality and dwelling speculatively on his intentions. An example comes from the *Observateur anglais* article of 1778 which made mention of Sade's habit of distributing spiked sweets to his sexual conquests: 'Il avait empoisonné tous les bon bons qu'il distribuait.'[22] In fact, the sweets were impregnated only with the aphrodisiac catharides, but we may notice that murder rather than sex is the motivation most readily attributed to the Marquis.

The linking of rapacious sexual appetite with mortal consequences is seen again in the following paranoid account of contemporary sexual mores by the conservative eighteenth-century historian Bachaumont: 'Plusieurs personnes sont mortes des excès auxquels elles se sont livrées dans leur priapisme effroyable.'[23] Such is the close association between the name of Sade and the idea of sexuality that kills that at the end of the eighteenth century the link is made between the reading of Sade's violent pornography and the act of sexual murder itself. Pierre Jean-Baptiste Chaussard comments: 'Qu'on interroge, avant de les conduire à la mort, les assassins qui, dans ce dernier temps, ont épouvanté la nature par de nouvelles cruautés. Ils vous diront sans doute que la lecture des ouvrages tels que *Justine*, *Aline* etc., que les représentations de ces pièces, dont les héros sont des brigands, ont alimenté et exalté leurs principes d'immoralité.'[24] These are early pre-echoes of the debate regarding the potentially dangerous effects of pornography in inciting criminal attacks. Moreover, the notion of 'copycat killings' raised here persists as a problematic of present-day sociological thinking.

Sade's perversions are the subject of another apocryphal and exaggerated anecdote published in the nineteenth-century memoirs of the Marquise de Créqui. She tells of workers on Sade's estate draining water from a pond where they had been forbidden to fish, only to make a shocking discovery: 'on vient d'y trouver le corps d'un jeune homme et celui d'une jeune fille, qui sont piqués comme des perdrix, la jeune fille avec du lard et le jeune homme avec des bouts de petits rubans nommés faveurs. Ils étaient attachés l'un à l'autre avec des nœuds de large ruban couleur rose.'[25] Here we have a glimpse of the way in which the image of the desecrated body, the sexualized corpse, as well as the rumour of the pleasure of murder, become indelibly linked to Sade's name. It is as much for such delirious fantasies of sexual murder associated with his name as for his pornographic novels and plays that Sade becomes a key player in the nineteenth-century imagination.

Indeed, it has been suggested that the sexually motivated killing described in Sade's works is a prototype of the phenomenon of sexual murder as we know it today.[26] This is easily understood when we look at such works as *Les Cent-vingt Journées de Sodome*, in the final section of which all the characters are killed in different ways by the four male libertines, so as to provide the ultimate orgasmic experience for the killers.

As Foucault will tell us, with characteristic gusto:

Le sadisme n'est pas un nom enfin donné à une pratique aussi vieille que l'Éros; c'est un fait culturel massif qui est apparu précisément à la fin du XVIIIe siècle, et qui constitue une des plus grandes conversions de l'imagination occidentale: la déraison devenue délire du cœur, folie du désir, dialogue insensé de l'amour et de la mort dans la présomption sans limite de l'appétit.[27]

Here Foucault speculates on Sade's historical import. While it is unlikely that this is the first moment at which such a taste would be found, what the available sources tell us is that at the end of the eighteenth century and the beginning of the nineteenth, Sade appears to serve a particular social and psychical function. He becomes an archetypal figure in the cultural—certainly the high-cultural—imagination. He symbolizes, both in the notoriety and elusiveness of his texts and in the mythical status of his persona, the birth of a rupture in aesthetic morality. The notion that crime, genius, sexual desire and death are intimately linked will remain a primary topos of art into the next century.

Encountering the Beyond

The relationship between lived experience and the content of art is extremely difficult to establish, particularly in a critical climate in which mimetic theories of art have been largely discredited. Nonetheless, the complex links between subjective and social reality in the texts of a given period must not be overlooked. We may wonder whether the many images of death and destruction in the literature in question were partially inspired by visible signs of mortality in the writers' environment.

Throughout the nineteenth century in France, death was a visible social reality to an extent that is largely unimaginable for twenty-first-century Westerners. In his study of nineteenth-century France, Theodore Zeldin tells us that the infant mortality rate was catastrophically high in comparison with other parts of Western Europe.[28] Moreover, poor sanitation and diet, as well as civil unrest, insurrections and the fallout of the Franco-Prussian war, meant that those who did survive infancy were unlikely to see old age. The existence of everyday memento mori is amply detailed in written accounts of the period. What is particularly relevant to us here is the way in which such encounters with death in life are narrated by contemporary artists.

In *Thérèse Raquin* (1867), Zola describes how a murderer, Laurent, makes daily visits to the morgue, in order to search for the missing drowned body of his victim. This becomes the pretext for a descriptive passage in which the morgue is presented as a social space: 'La Morgue est un spectacle à la portée de toutes les bourses, que se paient gratuitement les passants pauvres ou riches. La porte est ouverte, entre qui veut.'[29] Here, we see a version of the convention of death as social equalizer. Rich and poor lie side by side in their rigor mortis and, equally, the living rich and poor may walk among them free of charge. The spectacle of death becomes a diversion, an amusement for those 'amateurs' who pay a daily visit and are heard to applaud any new and particularly grotesque exhibits 'comme au théâtre'. Pleasure in death is unselfconsciously and volubly expressed.

Despite his melancholy reason for frequenting the morgue, Laurent himself is surprised by 'une sorte de désir peureux' on sight of a particularly attractive corpse:

son corps frais et gras blanchissait avec des douceurs de teinte d'une grande délicatesse; elle souriait à demi, la tête un peu penchée, et tendait la poitrine d'une façon provocante; on aurait dit une courtisane vautrée, si elle n'avait eu au cou une raie noire qui lui mettait comme un collier d'ombre: c'était une fille qui venait de se pendre par désespoir d'amour.[30]

The very conventional language of feminine sexual attractiveness is subverted here by the sudden fact of the hanged woman's deadness that comes in the mention of her contused throat. Just as the morgue is a space for all to walk in, so the corpses, displayed like meat or like whores, are available targets for every fantasy. Necrophilic pleasure becomes the currency of the masses, in its most oblique and its most literal senses. Indeed, the morgue is literally made to serve the purpose of the whorehouse, as we are told that 'C'est à la Morgue que les jeunes voyous ont leur première maîtresse'.[31]

Although *Thérèse Raquin* is a work of fiction, we have no reason not to trust Zola's Naturalist zeal for ethnographic detail in this case. Many journals and memoirs of the period make mention of the public accessibility of morgues, and described sightings of corpses are far from rare. Among the best known of these is an anecdote recounted in the *Mémoires* (1865) of Hector Berlioz (1803–69), in which he describes a Florentine *scène funèbre* which he claims to have witnessed.

Having seen a funeral cortège pass by, Berlioz follows the procession to the morgue where he pays in order to be allowed to enter the resting place and view the deceased. The spectacle is an impressive one: 'Une longue robe de percale blanche, nouée autour de son cou et au dessous de ses pieds, la couvrait presque entièrement. Ses noirs cheveux à demi-tressés coulaient à flots sur ses épaules, grands yeux bleus demi-clos, petite bouche, triste sourire, cou d'albâtre, air noble et candide ... jeune! ... jeune! ... morte! ...'[32] As one of the creators of the Romantic tradition, Berlioz describes the dead body in characteristic terms. The conventions of flowing, jet-black hair and white neck, found in many literary descriptions of beautiful women, are observed to the letter. However, chillingly, they are preceded not by a meticulous description of a grand robe in the style we will often remark in Balzac, but by the mention of a body-length shroud. The fact that this type of description of a beautiful woman is immediately familiar to a reader of Romanticism means that her deadness appears almost naturalized.

The articulation of her youth and her deadness is nonetheless expressive of agitation and excitement with its dramatic exclamation marks and sudden disjointed syntax, given by the *points de suspension*. This punctuation effectively suggests something missing, some suspension of comprehension. The mystery of death and the surprising revelation of its attractiveness are accounted for by this device.

The whole picture is one of voluptuousness and sadness mixed, reminding us of Baudelaire's assertion that beauty in a woman should leave the male spectator with the dual sentiment of sorrow and desire:

J'ai trouvé la définition du Beau, — de mon Beau. C'est quelque chose d'ardent et de triste, quelque chose d'un peu vague, laissant carrière à la conjecture. Je vais, si l'on veut, appliquer mes idées à un objet sensible, à l'objet, par exemple, le plus intéressant dans la societé, à un visage de femme. Une tête séduisante et belle, une tête de femme, veux-je dire, c'est une tête qui fait rêver à la fois, — mais d'une manière confuse, — de volupté et de tristesse; qui comporte une idée de mélancolie, de lassitude, même de satiété, — soit une idée contraire, c'est-à-dire une ardeur, un désir de vivre, associé avec une amertume refluante, comme venant de privation ou de désespérance. Le mystère, le regret sont aussi des caractères du Beau.[33]

Baudelaire could easily be describing Berlioz's experience before the corpse. A new notion of the sexual aesthetic is posited in both of these accounts. Here, beauty comes from something 'laissant carrière à la conjecture', something involving radical absence and the suspension of immediate understanding or classification. This signals a break with classical notions of beauty and suggests the presence of the Gothic, that is, of a twisted or tainted aesthetic. The appearance of death is seen to provide that Byronic touch of ruin that kindles a wantonness in beauty.

The idea of confusion, conjecture, indecision whether to mourn or whether to engage sexually are equalled in the experience of pleasurable dizziness Berlioz goes on to describe: 'La salle retentit du choc ... je crus que ma poitrine se brisait à cette impie et brutale résonance ... N'y tenant plus, je me jette à genoux, je saisis la main de cette beauté profanée, je la couvre de baisers expiatoires, en proie à l'une des angoisses de cœur les plus intenses que j'aie ressenties de ma vie.'[34] The tone of the piece narrates the experience of individual desire before the impenetrable mystery of death. The shock in the writing can be read as the *décalage* between individual emotion or perception and the material reality of the corpse, an object beyond rationalization. The presence of awe and the incomprehensible alongside beauty suggest the notion of the Kantian sublime. These authors are describing more than a sexual encounter: they are dressing Romantic ideas of the infinite in the language and imagery of sexual attraction. The idea of youth in death is seen as particularly striking, suggesting that it is this juxtaposition of unlikely characteristics which provides the shock spark of desire.

Although I do not wish to engage in speculative biographical criticism, it is worth pointing out that the youthful mortality rate did not only affect the impoverished, illiterate classes. The artists of the century often experienced losses that were then romanticized as the subject of art. Nodier's young lover met with premature death, prompting Pierre-Georges Castex to remark: 'C'est pourquoi sans doute, presque toutes ses héroïnes meurent jeunes, de langueur ou de désespoir; mais souvent aussi, à l'image de leur mort est associée la pensée de l'immortalité.'[35] Also, in her biography of Théophile Gautier,[36] Annie Ubersfeld emphasizes the significance of the death of his childhood sweetheart, Marie or Hélène. This young girl, who is thought to have died in pre-pubescence, is proposed as the prototype of the sexually attractive young dead women who are repeatedly resurrected in many of Gautier's *contes fantastiques*.

Similarly, we may call to mind Poe's marriage to his 13-year-old cousin Virginia, which soon ended in her death due to a ruptured blood vessel. Many critics hold that his relationship to this fragile girl was the more or less conscious inspiration for such tales as 'Ligeia'

(1838) and such poems as 'Annabel Lee' (1849), which have as their conceit a dead and resurrected female beloved.[37] Poe's resounding success among the French, often to the surprise of the English, may be seen to lie partly in his treatment of the themes of loss and mourning, which is unrelentingly intense and melodramatic.

Yet, even if there is some discrepancy between these romanticized portrayals of dead bodies as beautifully ethereal and the social realities of disease, death clearly was raw subject matter for many literary figures. The period March–November 1832 saw a cholera outbreak in France, the details of which are recorded in Antoine Fontaney's *Journal*, side by side with literary tittle-tattle from the salons. The following entry from 16 April casually juxtaposes a visit to the hospital morgue and a piano recital by Liszt:

Nous avons visité toutes les salles à peu près des hommes et des femmes, même celle du typhus. — Quelques-uns étaient bleus. — Tous ont l'air étonné et terrifié, les yeux profondément renfoncés et cerclés de noir. — Une pauvre femme avait les crampes. On la frottait cependant qu'elle criait misérablement. Une vieille femme toute violette montrait les dents. Nous avons rencontré en montant un mort qu'on descendait caché sous un drap. — On les range dans le caveau des morts dans leurs draps blancs chacun sur la terre. — On dirait des momies.
[...] Je vais chez Victor Hugo. — Liszt était au piano dans le salon. — Il nous joue une marche funèbre de Beethoven. C'était magnifique! Qu'il y aurait quelque chose de beau à faire là! Tous les morts du choléra se promenant à Notre-Dame avec leurs linceuls![38]

The horrific experience of the visit is recuperated and fed into an imaginative drama which elevates the fear and horror into an aesthetic experience.

This game of imaginative *what if?* is taken up again in the next entry. In the cemetery, Fontaney sees a covered coffin: 'c'était sans doute quelque belle et douce jeune fille ...'.[39] As before, a real object, here the coffin of an anonymous cholera victim, gives rise to an imaginative and libidinal fantasy. Fontaney creates from this spectacle a fictional alternative to reality. He inserts the ideal object beneath the opaque covering of the shroud. The vital tension between terror and prurient delight and the play between lived experience and the libidinal edge of imaginative drama in Fontaney's accounts are typical of the writing of the century.

The historian and diarist Alphonse Rabbe, whose reflections on the nature of life and death are posthumously collected in the *Album d'un pessimiste* (1835), draws attention to the paradox that fear should be the response to something that was not a stranger to the nineteenth century—the spectacle of death: 'Pourquoi ce nom de *mort* vous épouvante-t-il? N'avez-vous pas déjà vu sans pâlir et sans trembler quelques-uns de ses ouvrages dans les cimetières et dans les batailles? La mort n'a rien d'étrange, c'est une connaissance familière, nous la voyons tous les jours.'[40] It is perhaps not surprising that death should appear a daunting and shocking prospect to us in the early twenty-first century, given our relatively sanitized relationship with it (a relationship which has, however, become more intimate and threatening since the advent of AIDS). Yet Rabbe draws attention to the fact that however familiar one may be with it in the ordinary sense of the word, there will still be a relation of alienation and shock on contact with the idea of one's own death. There will still exist a complex system of associations which are hard to formulate and impossible to rationalize, and which constitute a relation to death that has more to do with internal emotional investment than the observation of social data.

Our relation will be marked by fear, and yet also, as Rabbe goes on to point out, by fascination and desire: 'La mort, quelque effroyable qu'elle soit, a des amants puisque beaucoup de malheureux la souhaitent. Oh! Quand pourra-t-elle m'éteindre de ses bras inflexibles et m'endormir dans le silence du cercueil!'[41] and 'Quand nos plus proches meurent, le désir de les suivre devrait être plus sensible que le regret de les avoir perdus.'[42] The vocabulary used in his musing on death suggests a concupiscence which, like the fear evoked earlier, goes beyond an immediate rational understanding. 'Amants', 'm'éteindre de ses bras' and 'le désir', coupled with the rapturous 'Oh!', suggest that the access to spectacles of death in the nineteenth century allowed for a particular type of emotional experience which, in the case of the writers discussed above, had its end point in art.

Necrophilia may well have been a preoccupation of the writing of the period because objects to stimulate desire for it were readily available in life. Factors such as the fashion for Romanticism, which doubtless affected the choice of the corpse as subject matter, and social factors such as the visible presence of the dead body, are not mutually exclusive. I have documented above several semi-factual accounts by nineteenth-century artists of encounters with corpses, which have much in common in terms of libidinal content and also in the choice of descriptive imagery and tone.

While it would be unwise to claim that any one century or culture had a particularly privileged or intimate relationship to death, I am positing that in nineteenth-century France there were various social factors which help to account for the documented fascination with necrophilia. A high incidence of sexualized dead bodies in art is not a coincidental phenomenon. Artistic content must be seen as a litmus paper of the fears, tastes and tendencies of a society. Local moments, historical events and contingent trends do not create but may make active or bring to the surface that which lies dormant in the human psyche. If Sade's post-revolutionary writings can be seen as the symptoms of a collective cultural trauma, then their nineteenth-century legacy suggests itself as the scars of a society caught between epochs, on the brink of an uneasy modernity. The need to exercise control over the maverick forces of sexuality and death, as well as to exorcize desire, is the intimate concern not only of imaginative writing but of the socio-medical discourses that establish themselves towards the end of the century.

The Pathologizing of Desire

The word 'necrophilia' enters the French and other European languages some decades after the artistic production discussed above. The term was coined by the Belgian alienist Joseph Guislain, and was first used by Jules Monneret in his *Treatise on General Pathology* (1861).[43] It was mentioned by Richard von Krafft-Ebing in the first edition of *Psychopathia Sexualis* (1886), the most famous work of nineteenth-century sexology, and filtered into the major European languages via subsequent translations of this work. It is certainly in frequent use in medical texts by the 1890s, and appears in the indexes of such texts as Charles Féré's *La Pathologie des émotions* (1892) and Max Nordau's *Entartung* (1892), as one of a group of taxonomies designed to describe the aberrant sexual tastes of the modern European subject.[44]

The vocabulary and intellectual frameworks for talking about sexuality that are today widely discussed, debated and, since Foucault, disputed in academic circles did not come into existence until the nineteenth century. Indeed, until the turn of the century, even the words 'heterosexual' and 'homosexual' did not exist.[45] 'Sexualwissen-schaft', translated as 'sexology',[46] was a branch of psychiatry that became prominent during the second half of the century with the aim of cataloguing the extensive range of sexual behavioural phenomena observed in contemporary clinical practice. As will be noted from the composition of the German word, emphasis was placed upon gaining scientific knowledge of the sexual realm. The idea that sexual impulses and behaviour were open to such study and understanding, and therefore were controllable, is central to this discourse and a facet of late nineteenth-century thinking. The forerunners of sexology, however, date back to experiments and theories developed earlier in the century.

The many epistemological breaks that occur within the burgeoning science of sexology are explicable in the light of fluctuations in law, as well as developing ideas regarding sickness, consciousness and the body. Gert Hekma details how the beginning of the nineteenth century in France marked a change in attitude from the punishment of perverted activity to the desire to examine the cause of the perversion.[47] Thus, the decriminalization of sodomy in 1800 meant that 'in 1843 three French doctors no longer examined the anus of a pederast's victim, but instead studied the mental state of the pederast himself'.[48] This climate, which encouraged searching within the practitioner's being for the seeds of his act, led to Heinrich Kaan's dissertation *Psychopathia Sexualis* (1844), which posits onanism as the source of all perversions. For Kaan, perversions were points along a continuum: once a human being engaged in masturbation, same-sex intercourse, bestiality and violation of a corpse might follow.

The perception that sexual fantasy was the first step towards acting out and illness was soon to change. In 1849, Michéa published 'Des déviations maladives de l'appétit vénérien', the starting point of which was a reported case of necrophilia (though the word did not yet exist). In this text, he displaced perversions as products of mental overactivity and relocated them as the results of physiological phenomena. Perverted behaviour was thus seen as a symptom of a morbid biological condition. It is possible to understand this detour, from Kaan's pre-psychopathological method to a re-centring on biological function, in the light of trends of thought in other branches of social and medical science of the period. The discussion of degeneration theory later in this chapter will provide an ideological context for the tendency to view deviant behaviour as a symptom of a pathology.

By the time Krafft-Ebing published *Psychopathia Sexualis*, the psychological and the physiological coexisted somewhat uneasily within sexological writings. Renate Hauser suggests that the various re-editions of *Psychopathia Sexualis* that appear throughout the 1880s and 90s place increasing emphasis on the psychological aspects of clinical observation of perversions. This suggests that Krafft-Ebing is ahead of his time and is a direct forebear, rather than an opponent of, his colleague and successor, Freud.[49]

Krafft-Ebing is certainly responsible for inaugurating many of the techniques used by modern sexology, principally that of the case study. This is the favoured method of articulation of sexology's key works, from *Psychopathia Sexualis* to such contemporary works as the Kinsey report. Long descriptive passages of the erotic imagination, often in the patients' own words, characterize *Psychopathia Sexualis*, and often very little discussion or analysis follows. Where there are attempts to account for the causal relations of aberrant behaviour, they are attributed mainly to conservative hereditary explanations.

Psychopathia Sexualis comprises case studies which fall into two main categories: first-person accounts in the confessional mode, and short biographical narratives intercut with clinical observation and occasional quotation from the subject's own verbal or written accounts. The literariness, and the prevalence of the erotic imagination and fantasy, are immediately in evidence and sit somewhat uneasily beside the sparse scientific claims.

The following passages were both found in the case history of the 'lust murderer' Vincenz Verzeni. The first is Krafft-Ebing's clinical summary:

He is twenty-two years old. His cranium is of more than average size, but asymmetrical. The right frontal bone is narrower and lower than the left, the right frontal prominence being less developed, and the right ear smaller than the left (by 1 centimetre in length and 3 centimetres in breadth); both ears are defective in the inferior half of the helix; the right temporal artery is somewhat atheromatous.[50]

The second is a quotation from Verzeni's confessions:

I had an unspeakable delight in strangling women, experiencing during the act erections and real sexual pleasure. It was even a pleasure only to smell female clothing. The feeling of pleasure while strangling them was much greater than that which I experienced while masturbating. I took great delight in drinking Motta's blood. It also gave me the greatest pleasure to pull the hair-pins out of the hair of my victims. (*PS* 89)

This latter account, a personal recollection of pleasure which lingers gleefully on the details of the act, is quite incongruous beside the long passage of physiological report. Krafft-Ebing's attempts to account for deviant fantasy and behaviour appear rather tame and ineffectual when read alongside the murderer's wilful mystification of his own acts and motives. There is a suspension of analysis and understanding in 'unspeakable delight', which draws attention to the difficulty faced by sexology in its self-imposed task of gaining scientific mastery of desire.

Consider the following extract:

> The story of a prelate [...] is of great interest as an example of necrophilia. From time to time he would visit a certain brothel in Paris and order a prostitute, dressed in white like a corpse, to be laid out on a bier. At the appointed hour he would appear in the room, which, in the meantime had been elaborately prepared as a room of mourning; then he would act as if reading a mass for the soul, and finally throw himself upon the girl, who, during the whole time, was compelled to play the *rôle* of a corpse. (PS 92)

Though brief and—unlike the previous quotation—failing to dwell on the pleasure of the act described, the account of the case has some of the qualities of a Sadeian scenario. The drama of the erotic scene is brought into focus, with its theatrical overtones of dressing up and role-playing. The details of the necrophilic fetish objects serve as a writerly build-up to the climactic moment of consummation. Part of the problem faced by the sexologist is that in describing and engaging with the erotic imagination, his own 'objective' position is inevitably put in question and he is to some extent implicated. At the very least, he is forced to play the dangerous role of storyteller.

Krafft-Ebing comments that the case of the prelate is 'of great interest as an example of necrophilia', but just what sort of interest is he suggesting we bring to our reading of his text? The 1901 English translation of the tenth German edition opens with the warning that this volume is only for the eyes of medical practitioners who may be instructed by it scientifically. The proscription is clearly in the interests of protecting those prurient readers who may be excited or corrupted by the inflammatory material within.

This cautionary measure seems to be suggesting two things. Firstly, it presupposes that doctors such as the author have such control over their own libidos that they are in no danger of being affected by such material. This implies the belief that knowledge (and, implicitly, class) brings with it the power of self-control as well as the right to exercise control over others. Secondly, a contradiction is revealed in the rhetoric of the work. Despite repeatedly explaining particular sexual perversions with recourse to the patients' individual medical histories and conditions, the prohibition suggests the awareness that such tendencies may be potentially universal and, on some level, intrinsic to the human condition. To prevent the average person from reading the work is to suggest that the acts and thoughts recounted may actually have a power to influence the imagination of those with different physiological make-up from that of the perpetrator described. Implicitly, then, the *bien-pensants* of the 1880s seem quite aware that these apparent aberrations have widespread affective power. In order to foil the prurient gaze of the uneducated into whose hands a copy of his book may fall, Krafft-Ebing sometimes renders the most obscene or extreme details of the case histories in Latin:

A man, fifty years of age, uses in a Lupanar only girls who clad in white, lie motionless, feigning death. He violated the body of his own sister, *immissione mentulae in os mortuae usque ad ejaculationem!* This monster had also fits of fetichism for *crines pubis puellarum*, and the trimmings of their fingernails; eating them caused strong sexual emotions. (*PS 92*)

This modest detour into Latin again strikes a jarring note with the acts described and the ecstasy their agents are said to experience. The word 'pleasure' occurs more times than I could count in this work and, despite the methods he employs to sanitize the material, Krafft-Ebing does not succeed in reducing it to dry clinical observations. The form of the narratives and confessions does not allow for this, and the case histories retain emotional and erotic intensity and remain disturbing for the reader.

Moreover, it is ironic that Krafft-Ebing should comment on Sade's writings in a footnote, where he states that 'fortunately it is difficult to-day [*sic*] to obtain copies' (*PS 95*). The fear that Sade's work might corrupt was, as we have seen, widespread. However, Krafft-Ebing's cautious censoring of his own work suggests that, despite the many claims of scientific objectivity he made, he fears that there may be little affective difference between Sade's pornographic writings and his own text.

The discourse of sexology harnesses the rhetoric of sickness and pathology, and the authoritative weight of morality, in an attempt to tame the raw material of excessive sexual and destructive desire. Yet the tension between fascination and desire on one side, and the urge to 'tidy up', categorize and morally condemn on the other, is never fully resolved. The stuff of Sadeian narrative is never fully contained by scientific encoding, and the prurient reader is never fully distinguishable from the careful scientific commentator.

Although I have pointed to aspects of hypocrisy in Krafft-Ebing's simultaneous conservatism and prurience with regard to the material he describes, it is also true that works like *Psychopathia Sexualis* demonstrate an opening up of the world of internal desire, an externalization of the hidden currents of mental life. Krafft-Ebing encouraged people to contribute case material, meaning that, for the first time, the pleasures of the mind and body were made articulable for ordinary people. There is something at least potentially revolutionary and forward-looking in this willingness to discuss sexuality and lay bare the erotic imagination. Moreover, the debates of the day bear witness to the shift from seeing sexuality in purely biologistic terms to the development of the psychiatric model that deals with the discrepancy between the internal world of desire and physiological reality.

The real problem lies in the fact that Krafft-Ebing's case studies do not stand free of moral or ethical judgement. Fantasies and behaviour are measured against a yardstick of normalcy, dressed as 'the natural'. Just as for Sade, the concept of nature was the truffle after which the sexologists went sniffing. However, unlike Sade, who strove to claim that nothing is unnatural, the sexologists classed almost everything as pathological. The result is that the texts read as extremely fearful, even while dwelling in loving detail on the most destructive and unusual flights of fantasy.

Regardless of how one interprets the ideological underpinnings of sexology, it is clear that it led to radical changes in the range of conceptual apparatuses with which to talk about sexuality. While there is evidence of a residual unease about the notion of plural sexual identities and desire structures, the case history gave ordinary people a chance to expose the extraordinary furnishings of their fantasy world. Also, through these innovations, psychological and emotional factors slowly came to prominence in the analysis of sexual life.

Degenerative Forces

The interest in morbidity, which we have observed in the arts and psychological sciences in the nineteenth century, filtered into a new social science—degeneration theory—which was influential in France and elsewhere in Europe for much of the second half of the century. Since the theory touches on certain issues adjacent to this project, I shall briefly examine some of its central tenets below.

Popularized in the 1840s in France by such medical thinkers as

Bénédict Morel (1809–73) and Philippe Buchez (1796–1866), degeneration theory considered that the evolution of the species and its intertwining with culture had reached an impasse. Focusing on the supposedly growing phenomena of prostitution, criminality and cretinism, as well as sexual and social deviancy, the degeneration theorists had a wholly pessimistic view of their contemporary historical moment. They saw it as a point at which the species was, increasingly with every new generation, regressing towards its atavistic roots. Just as necrophilia in literature can be seen as the underside of Balzac's portrayal of societal growth and positing of 'énergie vitale' as the creative source, so degeneration provides a counter-current to such influential production as Darwin's theory of evolution and Bergson's treatise on creativity.[51]

Degeneration theory serves as evidence that the nineteenth century was also prone to philosophical pessimism and fear. The fear in question centred on the idea that man was regressing towards an atavistic genus which lay inherent within him, and which must be fought against and controlled from without by state and science. The central belief of degeneration theory—that the human genus must tend towards eventual decay—can be seen as an echo of the nineteenth-century discovery of the second law of thermodynamics. The law of increasing entropy holds that the available energy of any closed system will inevitably decrease over time. This idea, displaced from science and re-applied to human development, has had tremendous suggestive power for many subsequent thinkers. George Steiner cites Lévi-Strauss's telling pun that 'our view of history is not an anthropology but an "entropology"'.[52]

Among the first in France to speak of *dégénerescence* was Morel in his *Traité de dégénérescences physiques, intellectuelles et morales* (1857). Morel's concept of degeneration was of hereditary deviation from the norm, which was manifest in the deterioration of both physical and moral faculties. Physical signs of degenerative disease, such as hernias, scrofula and club foot, were inextricable from intellectual and emotional disturbances resulting from such aberrant abuses as alcohol, tobacco and opium, not to mention the reading of morbid or Romantic literature. The deterioration of the human species and that of civilization were seen as linked and inevitable. The growth of urban populations and the rise of the masses were seen as noxious social symptoms, the only cure for which, according to Morel, was a 'moralization' of the masses.

This opinion is shared by Taine, critic, theorist and writer, lauded by the Goncourts and famed for his dictum 'j'ai horreur de la foule'. Daniel Pick, in his recent book on degeneration, points out that Taine's writing during the 1870s–1890s can be seen as linked to the period's crisis in social optimism.[53] Taine's work comprises a 'psychopathology of the revolution' (*FD* 68), taking the events of 1870 and 1871 and considering not only their immediate causes but the inheritance of degeneration which led to them. The effects of war are considered not only for those who lived through it but for future generations, so that the consequence of the human species undergoing a period of civil unrest would be a future crisis of greater magnitude.

The term 'Entartung', translated into English as 'degeneration' and into French as 'dégénerescence', was coined by Max Nordau in *Entartung* (1892). His work follows on from, and owes much to the work of, Morel, Charcot and the other French theorists discussed above. In it, he argues that civilization had fallen prey to a terrible crisis of disease caused by the rupture between the human body and social conditions. Madness, suicide, crime and morbid or Decadent literature were all symptoms of this modern disease: 'We stand now in the midst of a severe mental epidemic; of a sort of black death of degeneration and hysteria.'[54] Nordau's rhetoric is extreme and hyperbolic here, as in 'the world of civilisation is an immense hospital ward'.[55] The danger of social change is figured by analogy with organic disease and death, so that the shadow of the dying or dead body stands in for the end of civilization as a whole. Reading the rhetoric of these theorists, one gains the impression that the human organism and ordered society were facing imminent demise.

There is a sense that the theory of natural selection, without being an incorrect model, was failing to account for the poverty, social unrest, crime and discontent that seemed prevalent in society. However, equally, it would be wrong to see degeneration theory as the absolute antithesis of evolution, which would be logically a condition of stasis, an evolutionary impasse. Structurally, the theories work in exactly the same way, with one progressing and the other regressing. Through an early twenty-first-century lens, we can see the quantifiable phenomena of degeneration—the increasing racial mixture within society, the demographic centralization that took place in the mid-twentieth century, the divergence of sexual orientation—as a sort of progress or evolution towards a liberal modern moment. In the eyes of the conservative degeneration theorists however, this interpretation would have been unthinkable.

It would be possible to imagine evolution and degeneration as necessary dialectical forces of history. In his *Lectures on the Philosophy of Religion*, Hegel shows how a degenerative social climate could mark a necessary historical turning point for social progress. His discussion of the Amazonian warriors posits that, in order to reach our epoch of patriarchal 'civilization', we had to transcend the historical drama of savage matriarchy. In this model, the degeneration of the populace would exist as a necessary historical staging post, which would allow regenerative (and 'higher') social forces to rise in their wake. The metaphor of cyclical birth and decay is refused, however, by the pessimistic philosophical tendencies of the period.

The language of degeneration, as we have seen, relies on metaphors of nosology and pathology. The degeneration of the individual psychiatric patient and the society as a whole, or the organic body and the body politic, become interchangeable echoes of each other. Another example of this way of thinking which posits a parallel between the microcosm and the macrocosm is the idea that the sexuality of the human species must have developed in the same way as an individual infant.[56] It is perhaps at this moment that the sexual becomes actively acknowledged as a symptomatic facet of the social. The logical outcome of this way of thinking is to interpret unusual or unorthodox behaviour as pathology, and any case of deviance as a symptom of a greater social ill. The metaphorical structure linking body and body politic is thus collapsed and radically literalized.

Degeneration theory, then, can be said to operate according to a phantasy of necrophobia—a fear of death and the dead body—at the social level. Death is assumed to be the end for these commentators (historically located, as they are, after Nietzsche's proclamation of the death of God), and Hegel's model of historical regeneration is negated. Necrophobia, in this sense, acts as a conservative force, stemming change and petrifying the existing order. Death, after all, represents the absolute change of state (change in the State). This formula is complex and paradoxical. An urge to memorialize and fossilize the past would more immediately be recognized as a necrophilic impulse than a necrophobic one. In fact, I would argue that the two must necessarily coexist, following Freud's contention that repulsion and attraction are two sides of the same emotional coin. The psychopathology of the age can be characterized by a necrophilic–necrophobic tension at the level of shared unconscious phantasy. Evolution and degeneration, logical partners in the cycle of death and rebirth, become dislocated and untethered as they are made into highly charged talismans onto which, respectively, hope and fear may be projected.

The Degenerate Voice of Literature

The portrayal of crime and sexual dissidence is predominant in the literature of the century in France and England alike. Balzac's realist tales of the Parisian *monde*, not the texts we would usually associate with Decadent subject matter, are, in fact, intercut with allusions to the shadowy world of crime, passion and murder.[57] Zola's *Rougon-Macquart* cycle attempts to take the dual voice of scientist and transgressive experimenter, at once analyst of and participant in the murders of *La Bête humaine* and Nana's fatal charms. This privileged role of the author, which allows for simultaneous scientific scrutiny and vicarious *jouissance*, can be seen as part of the reason why the degeneration theorists objected so strongly to literature of this type, even if they formulated their objections on scientific grounds. Zola, in particular, was vilified by Nordau: 'Does he think that his novels are serious documents from which science can borrow facts? What childish folly!'[58]

I have defined degeneration as the structural intellectual space in which fear of the future and the unknown may be articulated. To a certain extent, writers can be seen to sidestep the fear of impotence manifest in the writing of the theorists. In their role as creators, they can choose what of social theory to incorporate and what to leave behind, what to comment upon and what to transform into beauty. Their creation of an alternative world is perforce affected by the intellectual and emotional currents that touch them, but the site of artistic production also provides a space for a cathartic working through of desires and fears. Writing is thus the subject matter of theory and an alternative to it. The similarity in the fear and fascination of the individual before the spectacle of death (see my discussion of Berlioz, Fontaney and Rabbe on pp. 26–30 above), and the fear and fascination of the theorist of sexology and degeneration before the spectacle of moral decay, cannot be ignored.

The schizophrenic split voice is reminiscent of Robert Louis Stevenson's *Strange Case of Dr Jekyll and Mr Hyde* (1886). In this famous work, the idea of the degenerate seed contained within the seemingly flourishing civilized entity is fully explored. The rhetorical device we have noted throughout of taking the part for the whole, and vice versa, is nicely encapsulated in this work. The figure of Jekyll/Hyde can be seen to stand in for the whole society cleft in two by the perceived dual attractions of sexuality and culture. Also it may emblematize the writer's role as doctor and patient, observer and observed, superego and id. The split subject created is both a product of a sickening modernity and a portrait of the nineteenth century's growing interest in the complex nature of identity and in the relationship between the subject and the environment.

We have seen how writing about necrophilia in the nineteenth century may be simultaneously a way of re-encoding personal dramas of loss, bereavement and the fascination of death, and a means of playing on the social fears of the day. The alliance of the poetic persona with death—the adoption of a necrophilic position—is a way of demarcating, in the most extreme way, the marginal emotional and political territory which the artist maps out for her/himself in the nineteenth century. Following in the wake of Sade's libertine and Romanticism's noble criminal, the necrophilic writer elevates her/his aesthetic sensibility to the status of a cult, and we can suppose that s/he performs her/his artistic task with an equal mixture of self-purging and conscious manipulative intention.

The tendencies observed within the disciplines and theories examined above have revealed two major currents. Firstly, sexology and degeneration theory reveal the desire to expose the internal world of sexual imagination and fantasy and to establish a body of knowledge about them that may be used to control social behaviour and stem the tide of moral degeneration. Thus, there are signs of apparent liberalism in encouraging the expression of desire, yet ultimately the knowledge gained from such revelation would be used for the purposes of control.

Secondly, a counter-current is visible, which can in part be seen as an unintended result of the first. The rallying cry of sexology to investigate the erotic imagination of the human subject is contemporaneous with a proliferation of articulations of desire in art and literature. Krafft-Ebing's scientific work and Sade's novels alike contain fantasies of a disturbing and extreme nature which are seen to touch the sensibilities of those who come into contact with them. Within the artistic community, Sade's works are re-digested and his reputation revived. He is seen to be capable of providing a vision of aesthetic and sexual rebellion with relevance for the nineteenth century. Simultaneously, death becomes the subject of imaginative fantasy, as both a sexualized object and a facet of social reality recast in fiction.

In the light of the nineteenth-century cholera plague and bloodshed, the idealization and sexualization of the dead body can be seen as a striving to overcome a fearful reality embodied in the social sphere. It can also be seen as the attempt to achieve the re-personalization of death as a fantasized friend, lover or comforter, as seen in Baudelaire's lines:

> C'est la Mort qui console, hélas! et qui fait vivre;
> C'est le but de la vie, et c'est le seul espoir.
> ('La Mort des pauvres', *OC* i. 126)

Almost a century later, a conceptual term is coined to express the human subject's desire for death. Freud's theory of the 'death drive', which posits, in a formula similar to Baudelaire's above, that death is 'the aim of all life', will come under discussion in the following chapter.

Notes to Chapter 1

1. Gilles Deleuze and Félix Guattari, *L'Anti-Œdipe* (Paris: Minuit, 1972), 36.

2. Such as the study undertaken by Richard Cobb, *Death in Paris: The Records of the Basse-Geôle de la Seine, October 1795–September 1801, Vendémiaire Year IV–Fructidor Year XI* (Oxford: Oxford University Press, 1978).

3. Praz devotes a chapter of *The Romantic Agony* to Sade's influence on the century's libidinal imaginative preoccupations. George Blin's *Le Sadisme de Baudelaire* (Paris: Corti, 1948) looks at Sade's influence on this writer. Other examples include Maurice Blanchot, *Lautréamont et Sade* (Paris: Minuit, 1963); Douglas B. Saylor, *The Sadomasochistic Homotext: Readings in Sade, Balzac and Proust* (New York: Peter Lang, 1993), and Scott Carpenter, *Acts of Fiction: Resistance and Resolution from Sade to Baudelaire* (University Park: Pennsylvania State University Press, 1995).

4. However, other examples of eighteenth-century textual necrophilia can be found. At the end of Prévost's *Histoire du chevalier des Grieux et de Manon Lescaut* (1731), the eponymous hero spends delirious days in the desert with his lips pressed against those of the dead Manon, his object of obsessive desire.

   Necrophilia is also the conceit and the figure for love and desire in a poem by Louis-Sébastien Mercier, *Lettre de Dulis à son ami* (Paris: La Veuve Duchesne, 1767). The poem includes a scene in which a young man comes to be watching over the corpse of a beautiful girl whom he recognizes as his former lover, betrothed to another in an arranged marriage. Dulis's mounting desire and the moment of consummation are described with some pudeur (p. 25):

Je m'élance ... Tout fond dans la nuit du trépas
Je me lève agité, tremblant, hors de moi-même.

Necrophilic content is diminished by the fact that the beloved, Junie, is not dead after all and awakens to find herself pregnant after this would-be posthumous violation (reminding us of Heinrich von Kleist's *Die Marquise von O*). The pregnancy, however, leaves us in no doubt that the sexual act took place. Thus in Mercier's poem, necrophilia is repudiated even as it is announced as the act of an overwhelming desire. What is most interesting is that it becomes a figure or narrative device for suggesting the workings of extreme passion. I am grateful to Edward Nye for drawing my attention to this little-known eighteenth-century work.

5. Quoted in Andrzej Siemek, *La Recherche morale et esthétique dans le roman de Crébillon fils* (Oxford: Oxford University Press, 1981), 34–5.

6. *Les Cent-vingt Journées de Sodome*, in Sade, *Œuvres*, ed. Michel Delon, 3 vols., Pléiade (Paris: Gallimard, 1990), i. 275.

7. Ibid., i. 373.

8. The appearance of the Pléiade edition of Sade in 1990 is perhaps the ultimate example of this canonization.

9. Charles-Augustin Sainte-Beuve, 'Quelques vérités sur la situation en littérature', *La Revue des deux mondes* (July 1843), 14.

10. Jean-Jacques Pauvert was prosecuted for having published *La Philosophie dans le boudoir*, *La Nouvelle Justine*, *Juliette* and *Les Cent-vingt journées de Sodome*.

11. Gustave Flaubert, *Correspondance*, ed. J. Bruneau, 4 vols. (Paris: Conard, 1910), i, 1831, p. 52.

12. Gustave Flaubert, *Souvenirs, notes*, ed. Chevally Sabatier (Paris: Buchet et Chastel, 1965), 1841, p. 70.

13. Edmond and Jules de Goncourt, *Journal 1863* (Apr. 1860), ed. R. Ricatte (Paris: Fasquelle et Flammarion, 1959), 730.

14. For further information on this point, see Nick Harrison, *Circles of Censorship* (Oxford: Oxford University Press, 1995). Harrison underlines the difficulty of tracing Sade's readership in the nineteenth century and points out that since reading Sade carried a certain kudos, many may have claimed to have read him who in fact had not.

15. *Journal 1849–60* (Mar. 1850), ed. Paul Viallaneix, 3 vols. (Paris: Gallimard, 1962), ii. 92.

16. Pétrus Borel, *Mme Putiphar* (Paris: Régine Desforges, 1972), 322.

17. Goncourt, *Journal*, 1196.

18. Jules Lemaître, *Les Contemporains* [1885] (Paris: Lécène et Oudin, 1887), 329.

19. Joseph Abraham Bénard, *dit* Fleury, *Mémoires*, ed. Laffite, 1835–6, cited by Basil Guy, 'Sur les traces du divin marquis', *Studi francesi* 14 (1970).

20. Flaubert, *Correspondance*, i. 51.

21. On Easter Sunday 1768, Sade flagellated the beggar Rose Keller at his house in Arcueil.

22. Pidansat de Mairobert, *L'Observateur anglais, ou Correspondance secrête entre Milord All'eye et Milord All'ear* (London 1778) iii. 67. Cited by Delon, introduction to Sade, *Œuvres*, p. xvi.

23. Louis Petit de Bachaumont, *Mémoires secrètes pour servir à l'histoire de la république des lettres*, 36 vols. (Paris: Librairie des Auteurs, 1866), i. 187.

24. Pierre Jean-Baptiste Chaussard, *Le Nouveau Diable boîteux: tableau philosophique et moral de Paris*, 2 vols. (Paris: Buisson, 1798–9), ii. 173–4.

25. La Marquise de Créqui, *Souvenirs de 1710–1800* (Paris, 1840), iii. 111–12. Cited by Delon, introduction to Sade, *Œuvres*, p. xx.

26. In their feminist sociological analysis of sexual murder, *The Lust to Kill* (Cambridge: Polity, 1987), Deborah Cameron and Elizabeth Frazer posit that the sort of criminal phenomenon termed sexual murder came into being as the specific cultural phenomenon we know today only towards the end of the eighteenth century (see p. 54). They point out the fallaciousness of giving something a name which implies a range of socio-historical codes and signs that are not meaningful in the context of the relevant century. They posit that destructive crime has been seen to bear an aesthetic dimension and transcendental philosophical potential only since the writings of Sade.

27. Michel Foucault, *Folie et déraison: histoire de la folie à l'âge classique* (Paris: Plon, 1961), 437.

28. See Theodore Zeldin, *France 1848–1945*, 2 vols. (Oxford: Clarendon Press, 1973–7), ii. 968–71.

29. Émile Zola, *Thérèse Raquin* (Paris: A. Lacroix, 1876), 100.

30. Ibid., 101.

31. Ibid., 103.

32. Hector Berlioz, *Mémoires* [1870], 2 vols. (Paris: Garnier-Flammarion, 1969), i. 274. For the full description of the funerary scene, see i. 273–5.

33. Charles Baudelaire, *Œuvres complètes*, ed. Claude Pichois, 2 vols., Pléiade (Paris: Gallimard, 1975–6) [OC], i. 657.

34. Hector Berlioz, *Mémoires*, i. 275.

35. Pierre-Georges Castex, *Le Conte fantastique en France de Nodier à Maupassant* (Paris: Corti, 1951), 125.

36. Annie Ubersfeld, *Gautier* (Paris: Stock, 1992), 17.

37. For a thorough account of mourning and the female corpse in Poe's life and works, see Bronfen, *Over her Dead Body: Death, Femininity and the Aesthetic* (Manchester: Manchester University Press, 1992), 326–36, 366–7.

38. Antoine Étienne Fontaney, *Journal intime* (Paris: Presses françaises, 1925), 132–3.

39. Ibid., 134.

40. Alphonse Rabbe, *Album d'un pessimiste* [1835] (Paris: Presses françaises, 1924), 71.

41. Ibid., 73.

42. Ibid., 75.

43. According to Alexis Épaulard in *Nécrophilie, nécrosadisme, nécrophagie* (Lyons: A. Storck, 1901).

44. For a recent, detailed account of the incorporation of this and other names of perversion types into French, see Vernon A. Rosario, *The Erotic Imagination: French Histories of Perversity* (Oxford: Oxford University Press, 1997).

45. The first German usage of these terms was in a letter from K. M. Kertbeny to Ulrichs. In 1892, J. Kiernan used 'heterosexual' to refer to those with 'inclinations to both sexes'. The translation of Krafft-Ebing's *Psychopathia Sexualis* into English in the same year established the meanings with which we are familiar today. (Rosario, p. 178)

46. Iwan Bloch (1872–1922) is believed to have coined the term.

47. Gert Hekma, 'A history of sexology: social and historical aspects of sexuality', in *From Sappho to de Sade: Moments in the History of Sexuality*, ed. Jan Bremmer (London: Routledge, 1991), 173–93.

48. Ibid., 176. Hekma's source material for this assertion is Ferrus, Foville and Brierre de Boismont, 'Attentat aux mœurs', *Annales médico-psychologiques* 1 (1843), 289–99.

49. See Renate Hauser, 'Krafft-Ebing's psychological understanding of sexual behaviour', in *Sexual Knowledge, Sexual Science*, ed. Roy Porter and Mikulás Teich (Cambridge: Cambridge University Press, 1994), 210–27.

50. Richard von Krafft-Ebing, *Psychopathia Sexualis* [*PS*], trans. of 10th Ger. edn. by F. J. Rebman (London: Rebman, 1901), 87.

51. Henri Bergson, *L'Évolution créatrice* [1907] (Geneva: Skira, 1945).

52. George Steiner, *On Difficulty and Other Essays* (Oxford: Oxford University Press, 1978), 186.

53. See Daniel Pick, *Faces of Degeneration* (Cambridge: Cambridge University Press, 1989) [*FD*], 67.

54. Max Nordau, *Degeneration* [1892], trans. of 2nd Ger. edn. by George L. Mosse (London: Heinemann, 1895), 537.

55. Max Nordau, *Conventional Lies of our Civilisation*, trans. of 7th Ger. edn. by George L. Mosse (London: Heinemann, 1895), 1.

56. The Hegelian idea of chronological primitivism, which holds a child's sexuality to be comparable to that of primitive man, is seen in Kaan's *Psychopathia Sexualis* (Leipzig, 1844) and picked up by Krafft-Ebing in the later work of the same name. The sexologists believed that the history of mankind's sociality and sexuality must have followed stages of development analogous to a child's sexual development.

57. See, among others, *Sarrasine* (1830), in which gender identity and heterosexuality are put into question and undermined; *Ferragus* (1833), where the two worlds meet in the figure of the rehabilitated ex-confidence trickster; *La Fille aux yeux d'or* (1834–5), where incest and debauchery lead to murder; and *Le Père Goriot* (1834), featuring the figure of Vautrin, the gentleman criminal.

58. *Degeneration*, 489. For a discussion of Zola as a serious degeneration theorist, see Pick, *Faces of Degeneration*, 74–96.

CHAPTER 2

Immobilizing Impulses:
Death in Psychoanalysis

Hermann me dit : Je songe aux tombes entr'ouvertes!
Et je lui dis: Je pense aux tombeaux refermés!
VICTOR HUGO, 'À quoi songeaient les deux cavaliers dans la forêt'

Sexual perversion is the subject of the first of Freud's *Three Essays on the Theory of Sexuality* (1905).[1] This is appropriate for several reasons. Firstly, it situates Freud in the tradition of sexology, which has consistently taken as its object of study the diversity of human sexual expression. Secondly, it emphasizes that perversion must be of primary concern to the psychoanalyst, since it both describes the character of the child's erotic development and is an adult psychical phenomenon every bit as inevitable as 'normal' sexuality. The importance that Freud attributes to perversion will be matched by subsequent analysts; indeed, perversion studies continues to constitute a lively area of theorization and debate within psychoanalysis, as evidenced by the extensive bibliography of recent texts on this subject.[2]

While sexuality is an early concern of Freud's work, the question of death, perhaps appropriately, takes precedence towards the end of his career. It is with the later writings on masochism and the controversial discovery of the 'death drive' that the focus of investigation and interest turns to questions of death, negativity and nihilism. Freud sets out to discover the mechanisms of humankind's search for survival, sexual satisfaction and reproduction, but increasingly he finds his attention drawn to the tendency of the human organism to seek out its own destruction. In 1920, Freud reached the pessimistic conclusion that the subject wants, not only to die, but 'to die only in its own fashion' (*Beyond the Pleasure Principle*, SE xviii. 3–64, 39). The ambitious self-determinism suggested by this formula is striking.

In the short paper 'On Transience' (1916), we find an allegorical address to the problem of conceiving of death from within life. Here, Freud recounts an anecdote of a country walk with a friend who expresses his distress in the face of the inevitable decay of the beautiful landscape. This prompts Freud to wonder how a flower, or any beautiful object, can induce awe and appreciation in us, when we know that is inevitably fated to die. Finally, he proposes the following response: 'A flower that blossoms only for a single night does not seem to us on that account less lovely' (*SE* xiv. 306). Although, on one level, Freud's response reinforces the triumph of life, the implicit suggestion behind these words is that impending absence may, in some way, be a factor in enhancing beauty. Doom adds that touch of piquancy which sharpens the experience of awe before beauty. This can be seen as approximating to the sentiment linked to the poetic tradition of *carpe diem*, which urges us to gather rosebuds while we may, or fêtes the beauty of a woman even though (implicitly because) she is doomed to fade and die.[3]

However, despite this gesture towards recognizing the mutual attraction of life and death, Freud concentrates mainly upon the conflict between them. This tendency is suggested in his positing of the dualistic psychical model of Eros and Thanatos, and his attempt to ascertain which of the two is primary, and which secondary. In this, he often overlooks the very factor to which he has drawn our attention in such texts as 'On Transience': their essentially complementary nature and its attendant complexities and ambiguities. This complicity is largely unspoken, and its frequent absence may be seen as the repressed content of Freud's discourse.

Beyond the Pleasure Principle is a groundbreaking text for Freud, which bears witness to certain re-formulations and advances in his thinking. It can also be read as a deeply personal and pessimistic text, echoing his sadness at the events of the First World War, and his frustration at his own worsening health. The text sets out to decentre previous Freudian assumptions quite radically: it challenges the hegemony of the pleasure principle, replaces pan-sexualism with a drive to return to the inorganic, and ultimately shifts the dualistic opposition of 'ego-instincts versus sexual-instincts' to a focus on 'life-instincts versus death-instincts'.

Freud's essay postulates that the wish to return to an earlier, inorganic state is the primary and most pervasive drive of the human psyche: 'We cannot escape a suspicion that we may have come upon the track of a universal attribute of instincts [...] which has not been [...] explicitly stressed. *It seems, then, that an instinct is an urge inherent in organic life to restore an earlier state of things* which the living entity has been obliged to abandon' (*SE* xviii. 36). Subsequent critics have attacked Freud for the apparently tautological assertion that all instincts behave like the death drive, seeking out an earlier state. We can understand this rather rhetorical assertion as Freud's attempt to show that the death instinct is not contrary to the other instincts but is merely in excess of them. It is an ur-drive. Freud goes on to tell us that the pleasure principle comes to serve the aims of the death instinct, contradictory though this may seem. By this, he means that the ultimately desirable state of the nirvana principle (the radical nothingness that is the aim of death drive) is ambiguously close to the pleasure principle (the reduction of tension to zero), which is usually linked to the aims of the life instinct. Both states are constituted by the removal of internal tension and antagonism.

This paradox appears also in the dynamic of the erotic, or at least in the masculine sexual imaginary. In the case of sexual excitement, an initial increase in tension is pleasurable. However, by desiring the culmination of the pleasure in climax, the subject seeks to put to rest this enjoyable tension. Since the aim of the act of sexual intercourse is orgasm, we can assume that this latter desire, which stills (kills) the pleasurable tension, is a stronger force than the desire to maintain excitement. From this we can observe that the very destruction of enjoyable sexual tension brings, even in 'normal' psychology, a pleasure all of its own, linked to the fall in erotic excitement. The post-coital state of temporary satiation is more comparable to death than to life.

According to Freud, the death drive should be understood as a dynamic principle in a hydraulics-based model, rather than as a literal death wish.[4] However, his choice of the emotive nomenclature 'Thanatos' means that we cannot help personifying this drive, attributing to it a meaning pertinent to our physical and metaphysical dramas. There is an irresistible temptation to read this essay as Freud's attempt to thematize the obsessions of his age.

As Freud began thinking towards this new theory of instinctual life, he was led to reconsider his ideas concerning masochism and sadism, and their relation to each other. His original position had been as follows: 'Clinical observations led us [...] to the view that masochism [...] must be regarded as sadism that has been turned round upon the subject's own ego' (*SE* xviii. 54). Now, however, he amends: 'Masochism, the turning round of the instinct upon the subject's own ego, would in that case be a return to an earlier phase of the instinct's history, a regression [...] there *might* be such a thing as primary masochism' (*SE* xviii. 55). This would suggest that Freud wants a destructive relation to the self to be understood as the foundation of psychical life. The radical aim of the death-driven masochistic child would be the self-inflicted cessation of life at the earliest possible opportunity.

Proving the existence of a death drive has been a problem for Freudian psychoanalysts, and the highly speculative and theoretical nature of *Beyond the Pleasure Principle* has led to many practitioners rejecting the concept altogether. As the memories of infantile nihilism are generally inaccessible to the adult patient, it is impossible to capture an instance of 'pure death drive' on the analyst's couch.[5]

Freud's later commentator and a defender of the death drive, Jean Laplanche, devotes a full-length study to these questions. In *Vie et mort en psychanalyse*, he demonstrates that the unconscious is incapable of conceiving of its own death. This means that the death drive is only ever visible when directed outwards towards another person: 'nous n'accéderions à quelque pressentiment de notre propre mortalité que dans l'identification ambivalente avec la personne chère dont nous souhaitons et redoutons la mort à la fois'.[6] Just as the child is forced by the impulses of survival to develop an anaclitic and later erotic dependency on the mother, so the suicidal drives come to rely on the agency of the other to achieve the aims of deflecting suicidal aggression. The unambivalent desire to return to the inorganic, which is Freud's initial definition of the death drive, is a characteristic of pre-verbal infant life only.

Laplanche explains that the original internalization of conflict comes during the period of deferral between the genesis of sexuality in the infant, and maturation when 'la passion' finds expression. This would mean that the death drive, embodied as aggression and frustration, is present not as one pole of conflict but as '*le conflit* substantialisé':[7] 'Ce qui se défend dans cette vue freudienne, c'est l'individu en lutte pour sa survie, survie qui serait menacée par la sexualité.'[8] Laplanche distinguishes sexuality (the principal instinct of psychoanalysis) from Eros. Eros is a binding and cohesive principle, holding sexual energy together, cathecting an object, while sexuality (or Thanatos) is radicalized as ultimately unbound energy, the negative of life.

He concludes: 'C'est que la pulsion de mort n'a pas d'énergie propre. Son énergie c'est la libido. Ou, pour mieux dire, la pulsion de mort est l'âme même, le principe constitutif, de la circulation libidinale.'[9] Ultimately, then, the death drive exists as the necessary concomitant of 'lively' sexuality: indeed, it is the conflictual knot of unbound sexuality itself. Leo Bersani comes close to the same idea in the chapter of *Baudelaire and Freud* in which he discusses death drive and sadism. He writes: 'The Freudian death instinct is a myth actually meant to account for the inherent sexuality of death—that is, for the profoundly exciting nature of the ultimate exceeding of quantative limits in the absolute "discharge" of death.'[10] This type of thinking, where two apparently distinct and even opposing terms are seen to share a common genesis, is not uncommon in Freud's work. In writing of female sexuality, Freud points out that a heterosexual, adult woman who has successfully arrived at genitality will positively desire a passive aim: 'There is only one libido, which serves both the masculine and the feminine sexual functions [...] we must not forget that it also covers trends with a passive aim' ('Femininity', *SE* xxii. 131). Just as libido, whether in the service of 'masculine' or 'feminine' aims, is seen to be genderless, so the conflictual couple of Thanatos and Eros may be seen to have a parallel sexual existence. Indeed, Laplanche tells us that Freud abandoned the idea of calling the energy fuelling the death drive 'destrudo', as a complement to the life drive's 'libido', in acknowledgement of the fact that they share the same energy source.[11]

However, if the death drive is by nature silent and invisible, it must require a vehicle other than itself in order to mobilize its energies and become visible. Hannah Segal, a champion of the death drive, tells us that death only ever manifests in clinical practice through a tension within the sexual sphere: that is, through perversion. Most commentators, including Segal, cite sadomasochistic phantasy and behaviour as the most likely outcome of such a fusion of Eros and Thanatos. However, necrophilia would seem an equally likely form for death-driven perversion to take. It may be, in fact, that 'necrophilia' is the most appropriate name available to us to describe death-driven perversion.

Towards a Psychoanalytic Theory of Necrophilia

Krafft–Ebing posited that necrophilia was a manifestation of sadism, involving a love of cruelty. His follower Moll contradicted him in 1912, stating that since the basic property of a corpse is that it is beyond the point of feeling pain or of suffering in any way, the infliction of cruelty would be irrelevant.[12] It is the idea of death that attracts the necrophile. Indeed, the increase of tension in a violent struggle may be repellent to him.[13] So although we may make certain links between the dynamic springs of necrophilia and sadism (as clinical perversions), the fact remains that the principal quality of necrophilia is that it involves not just a subjugated object, but a dead one.

Given the apparent prerequisite of radical immobility in necrophilia, one may draw an analogy with the dynamic model of fetishism established by Freud in his 1927 paper (*SE* xxi. 147–58). The fetish is an object, usually inanimate, which becomes invested with erotic interest and valued irrationally as a sexual object. In Freudian thought, the fetish object represents the desired phallus of the mother, split off and regained. It represents a double-edged, self-contradicting mechanism of disavowal and triumph: 'I know mother doesn't have a penis, but (because) here it is.'

Fetishism is, for Freud, the prototype of all perversions. In his phallic psychical economy, the spectre of castration has foundational status in the construction of (male) sexuality and subjectivity. Consider the following passage from 'The Medusa's Head':

To decapitate equals to castrate. The terror of the Medusa is thus a terror of castration that is linked to the sight of something. [...] The hair upon the Medusa's head is frequently represented in works of art in the form of snakes, and these once again are derived from the castration complex. It is a remarkable fact that, however frightening they may be in themselves, they nevertheless serve actually as a mitigation of the horror, for they replace the penis, the absence of which is the cause of the horror. (*SE* xviii. 273)

Here, as elsewhere, Freud suggests that fantasies and myths of violence and death, particularly by blinding and decapitation, are capable of provoking fear primarily because they suggest castration. While it may be true that castration is an imaginable loss for the subject, while death itself is unimaginable, surely this would mean that castration should be understood as a symbol of, or metaphor for, death itself, rather than the other way round? The knowledge that boys have a penis (that they might lose) comes after the forgetting of a primary relation to loss and absence. Without some primary awareness of the possibility of absolute death, the loss of the penis could not be imagined as irrevocable or devastating.[14]

In the case of necrophilia, we see the operation of a parallel mechanism to that which operates in fetishism. The disavowal of 'what I really know', discussed above, becomes an avowal of what the unconscious cannot know: 'I cannot die, and yet here is a dead other which I recognize as being different, yet with which I identify, therefore I know that one (I) can die.' The corpse is to the necrophile as the snakes of the Medusa's head are to the castration-anxious fetishist. The 'remembering' entailed by the encounter with death, however, is of a deeper and more primal sort than the spectre of fetishism.

Objectification is only the necessary condition of necrophilia in so far as the corpse represents the bodily, iconic proof of the abstract idea of radical absence. The perversion is Janus-faced in that it involves simultaneously a denial and an actualization of the ambitions of the ego. If fetishism is based on the dynamic of loss and disavowal of a part-object, then necrophilia is the fetish of entire loss, of complete absence. In positing this, I dream of a simultaneous knowledge and denial of the death of the self, which is equally feared and desired, and which has origins preceding the sphere of genital awareness. This would suggest that the source of desire is located outside of the erotic Oedipal configuration. A romance with death, rather than a family romance, may be the hidden heart of such perversion.

Despite my attempts to decentre somewhat the Freudian paradigm of Oedipus in conceptualizing the foundations of desire, I do not wish to downplay the importance of relationships with others in the formation of both 'perverse' and 'normal' sexuality. In order to conceive of death, the unconscious needs to recognize the other. We notice in formulations by Freud and Laplanche that the essentially auto-destructive drive is always turned outwards. The symbolic destruction of the self is achieved by proxy. The status of the other in Freudian, and more especially in Lacanian, psychoanalysis is of paramount importance. It comes as an intellectual inheritance from phenomenological philosophy, particularly that of Hegel. Death, the inconceivable other of life, is always imagined as the death of the other, a formulation which suggests a recognition of the potential of the death of the self projected out onto the other. Freud's Thanatos may come to serve the aims of the necrophilic perversion at the moment at which the drive is turned away from the self and, cathecting an other, becomes sexual desire. The other represents the wish for a sexual object and the wish for the death of the self, in some way combined.

Consciousness of self and other, according to psychoanalysis, functions by means of the psychical mechanisms of identification and projection. In *The Ego and the Id*, Freud tells us that it is impossible for the adult both to desire and to identify with the same object. He goes on to claim that this has not always been the case, and comments on a stage in the genesis of the subject: 'At the very beginning, in the individual's primitive oral phase, object-cathexis and identification are no doubt indistinguishable from each other' (*SE* xix. 29). Originally, then, the processes of desire and the need for self-recognition are the same. Laplanche has told us that in this remote infantile realm, the desire for sexual activity and the impossibility thereof lead the child to a surplus of aggressive, unbound energy that is the very heart of the death drive. Freud's sentence, quoted above, would suggest that originally we desire and identify with the same object, an object onto whom we focus aggressive sexual feelings. A desire to return to the inorganic, which according to *Beyond the Pleasure Principle* is the primary wish of the human subject, will be directed towards the undifferentiated dyad of self and other.

This observation of infantile drives would be consistent with our idea of necrophilia as the adult representation of wishes for the death of self, expressed through the agency of the other. Necrophilia, the desire for the dead other (as the iconic proof of the other's death), would appear a more primary perversion than the other perversions described in literature because it plays out an underlying wish to return to what one never was, to a state of non-being. In *Beyond the Pleasure Principle*, Freud tells us that 'all the organic instincts [...] tend towards the restoration of an earlier state of things' (*SE* xviii. 37–8) and '*inanimate things existed before living ones*' (38).

The very structure of necrophilia, according to our reading, is one in which identification and desire intermingle. It is a radically narcissistic type of desire, as its original object is neither mother nor father, but a concretization of the self's auto-destructive death wish. Following this model, necrophilia may be read as the natural resort of the libidinal adult who retains a keen sense of the originally self-focused death drive.

The structural model of necrophilic desire that I am proposing using psychoanalytic theory looks something like this:

1. Death drive = strongest drive in pre-verbal infantile life. Inability to distinguish between self and other. (Radically a drive to suicide.)

2. Maturation entails the formation of the unconscious and an awareness of the other. The unconscious is unable to conceive of its own death, so death drive meets libido and is directed towards an object.

3. Necrophilic perversion = the sexual desire to recognize my death through the other's death. May be sublimated, symbolized or fed into literary expression.

The implication, then, is that a profound need is met by the formulation 'the death of the other'. The image of the dead other in literature would be the nexus of a complex relation to self and object. The libidinal desire for the death of the other, in order to enjoy a vicarious recognition of one's own death, is one psychoanalytic definition we might propose for the dynamic underlying the perversion of necrophilia.

Mourning

I have argued so far, following Freud's logic which posits death drive as the underlying deep structure accounting for aggression and masochism, that necrophilia may be seen as a symptom or effect of symbolization by which the lure and fear of mortality are actualized in the world. The apparently universal fascination with spectacles of death, in life and in art (accident and murder scenes, dissections and post-mortems), would suggest that some degree of attraction to the dead operates in even apparently 'normal' human beings. One highly emotive circumstance which brings the individual into intimate contact with the dead is the case of bereavement. Mourning is one of the few contexts in which psychoanalysts have attempted to discuss necrophilia. In *On the Nightmare* (1931),[15] Ernest Jones claims that Oedipal guilt can be seen as one of the reasons why mourning, leading to psychic healing, may be impossible. For Jones, the dead we encounter always speak to us of our own parents, and we desire them in the name of our Oedipal allegiance. Jones posits that the common dramatis personae of the nightmare, such as the vampire, werewolf and witch, are pathological phantasy figures for dead parents. Such phantasies are analogous to dreams, in which disguised desires speak through mythical or hybrid figures. In this way, he proposes that the phenomenon of the nightmare is another manifestation of mourning as a perversion.

Marie Bonaparte's early psychoanalytic works on Edgar Poe's necrophilia follow a similar argument.[16] Bonaparte posits that Poe's prolific œuvre concerning love of the dead and an obsession with premature burial was a manifestation of the necrophilic love he felt for his dead mother. (Poe's mother died when he was aged 3, a prime Oedipal moment.) A dead mother would be unable to temper or repulse the son's incestuous love, so that the realization of the impossibility of Oedipal consummation would never be made conscious. Bonaparte thus proposes a model of necrophilia which is a variation of the classical Oedipal drama. Death is a mere vicissitude in the course of the family romance, and the driving force of Thanatos is overlooked. Below I shall consider ways in which our discussion of the death drive may impact upon theories of mourning.

The death of the other, real or fantasized, tends to be attended by feelings of intense, conscious guilt, loss and sorrow. Yet, as we have seen, the other is never a totally separate entity experienced as such. By means of the psychical processes of projection, incorporation and object cathexis, the other is intimately linked with and contained in the one. When someone close to us dies, it is our own relation to death that we are forced to confront. This is aptly illustrated by the opening lines of Nerval's well-known poem:

> Je suis le ténébreux, — le veuf, l'inconsolé,
> Le prince d'Aquitaine à la tour abolie:
> Ma seule *étoile* est morte — et mon luth constellé
> Porte le soleil noir de la Mélancolie.[17]

It is the beloved who is dead, yet the poetic persona himself is presented as diminished, wrecked, ruined. He inhabits death—symbolized by the ruined tower—by means of his consciousness of, and identification with, her death.

For Freud, successful mourning relies upon a person coming to terms with the absence of an other and relinquishing libidinal attachment. He explains:

Reality-testing has shown that the loved object no longer exists, and it proceeds to demand that all libido shall be withdrawn from its attachments to that object. This demand arouses understandable opposition [...] This opposition can be so intense that a turning away from reality takes place and a clinging to the object through the medium of a hallucinatory wishful psychosis. ('Mourning and Melancholia', *SE* xiv. 244)

Freud's theory of mourning posits 'melancholia' as the pathological response to loss. If the withdrawal of love from the absent figure does not occur, libido turns in on the subject's ego, where it establishes an identification, sometimes a suicidal one, with the lost object. Confusion may then occur for the subject between the traumatic pain of loss and the awareness of desire.

The subject must find ways of coping with the absence of the loved object, a fact which becomes apparent not only in actual death but, within childhood, in the first occurrence of the mother's absence which is experienced as a permanent loss. Freud's first observation in *Beyond the Pleasure Principle* centres on the compulsion to repeat, illustrated by the 'fort-da' incident of the child with his wooden reel. Freud proposes two interpretations of this incident, one being the instinct for mastery over the symbolic situation the child is seeking to represent: the absence of the (m)other: 'At the outset he was in a *passive* situation—he was over-powered by the experience; but, by repeating it, unpleasurable though it was, as a game, he took on an *active* part' (*SE* xviii. 16). This attempt at mastery might be supposed to serve the interests of the pleasure principle. However, the second interpretation proposed by Freud would not fit neatly with those aims: 'Throwing away the object so that it was "gone" might satisfy an impulse of the child's, which was suppressed in his actual life, to revenge himself on his mother for going away from him' (*SE* xviii. 16). These observations suggest the co-presence of the urge for mastery and the sadistic tendency in the psyche's management of loss. The excess of the desire for mother's presence, that which falls outside this comfortable formula, is the wish to make mother disappear at will, to orchestrate her absence. This can also be read as an echo of the earlier wish to make the self (now understood as self and mother) disappear.

Joseph Bierman's case study 'Necrophilia in a thirteen-year-old boy'[18] describes the analysis of a child who developed an obsessive preoccupation with the idea of becoming an undertaker. He turned this obsession, which arose after his sister's accidental death, into a game, almost like a young child 'playing at doctors'. Following Freud's 'fort-da' model, Bierman discusses this as the boy's attempt to turn the passive experience of his sister's illness, death and funeral into an active experience which he could control. Through his repeated game of 'undertaker', the boy was attempting mastery of the traumatic experience and fantasizing the maintaining of (posthumous) bodily contact with the other, the sister, for whom he experienced strong Oedipal feelings. I would add that through his identification with her, his own primary death wish was exacerbated, and then repeatedly played out.

In *L'Écorce et le noyeau* (1987), Nicholas Abraham and Maria Török describe a type of incorporation which may occur on the death of a loved one, the psychical aim of which is to 'refuser le deuil'.[19] The concept of introjection, introduced by Ferenczi, is defined as the psychical incorporation of an object or part-object in order to enlarge the ego. Török differentiates between 'introjection' and 'incorporation' by stating that the former is equated to a 'processus' and the latter to a 'phantasme'. This means that the original model of introjection is filling the empty mouth with food and, later on, with language. Incorporation, on the other hand, is seen as a phantasy of introjection, involving de-metaphorization and a shifting of suffering from the subject to the love object.

The chapter 'Deuil et mélancolie' explores the way in which, in order to deny the dreadful pain of loss and mourning, the psyche phantasizes having 'swallowed' that which has been lost: 'La "guérison" magique par incorporation dispense du travail douloureux du remaniement.'[20] Swallowing the loved object itself removes the necessity to 'swallow' (i.e. come to terms with) the loss and grief caused by their absence. No sense of pain or emptiness is experienced, as the object itself fills the psychical gap of mourning. This process is described as the forming of an intrapsychic crypt. This crypt has its own, unconscious, 'vie secrète' in which the needs and desires of the incorporated objects are indulged. In dreams and slips of the tongue, these desires may be given expression.

The case of a kleptomaniac boy is cited as evidence for these formulations. In analysis, he revealed that his compulsion to steal items of lingerie was an attempt to meet the demands of his dead sister who was an incorporated object. Further analysis revealed that the boy and his sister had enjoyed an incestuous sexual relationship.

The cases described above are extreme examples of the way in which psychical energy, mobilized in the service of the other, may often be serving the self's disguised or misplaced desire. The dead incorporated objects do not only fill the gap of real loss in the mind of the bereaved relative. They also serve an identificatory and libidinal function by acting as both other and part of self. I would argue that this uniquely allows the subject to fantasize and conceptualize her or his own death, in identification with the dead part of her- or himself. This may partially account for the reason why mourning is so intensely painful.

A work with particular relevance to this discussion is Serge

Leclaire's study *On tue un enfant*.[21] In this book, the Lacanian analyst asks why the death of a child—and more particularly the murder of a child—should be such an unbearable and taboo idea. He discusses case studies of analysands presenting fantasies and dreams of the murder of a child, attended by strong feelings of fear, guilt and desire. Leclaire posits that psychoanalysis has focused on the Oedipal phantasy of killing the father as a means of achieving adulthood and has ignored the more primary phantasy of killing the child.

The child to be killed, according to Leclaire, is the narcissistic phantasy of the parent's ideal child, the 'wonderful child'. As this phantasy has become part of the self, killing the child would also mean killing the self. Leclaire states: 'la logique du suicide découle d'un syllogisme parfait: pour vivre, il faut que je *me* tue'. [22] The wonderful child—me but also not-me—presents a logic close to the one I have been exploring. On one level, our perspectives are obviously different—I am attempting to trace the logic of death-driven perversion from a Freudian viewpoint, while Leclaire is suggesting a new approach within Lacanian clinical work. However a strong similarity is found in the attempts within both projects to decentre the traditional psychoanalytic emphasis on the cathexis to the parents and to foreground a primary relation to the self. In addition, Leclaire's project similarly stresses the importance of death drive as a foundation of psychical life. Leclaire states that not enough psychoanalytic works are prepared to take into account 'la force absolument contraignante de la mort nécessaire en chacun'.[23]

Having examined these Freudian and post-Freudian theoretical accounts of mourning and the failure to mourn, we see that the structures of loss they describe are central to the formulation of necrophilic desire. However, I would argue that those who theorize necrophilia as a perversion of mourning fail to take into account the part played by wishful identification with the dead, as a relic of primary death drive. Necrophilia mobilizes psychical energy in order to make a lost object return at will, but equally to enable a glimpse of self-loss in the perception of the other's death.

Denying the Desire for the Dead

Why is it that we have a wealth of literary examples of necrophilic desire and so little ready-made theorization, even if the theorists touch upon contiguous and analogous issues with considerable frequency? I would like to suggest that the same prohibition that operates in the subject's relation to the desire for the dead is echoed in the treatment of the subject in theoretical works. This avoidance of necrophilia *tout court* can be observed in the works of the sexologists, of Freud and of later writers. In *Psychopathia Sexualis*, Krafft-Ebing writes in the most emotive terms on the subject of necrophilia. He states that it is clearly an extreme and repulsive manifestation of a pathological condition:

Necrophilia: This horrible kind of sexual indulgence is so monstrous that the presumption of a psychotic state is, under all circumstances, justified [...] In any case, an abnormal and decidedly perverse sensuality is required to overcome the natural repugnance which man has for a corpse, and permit a feeling of pleasure to be experienced in sexual congress with a cadaver. (*PS* 580)

The emphasis is placed upon disgust, shame and morality rather than upon the desire to understand and analyse. Moreover, in several of Krafft-Ebing's other listed perversions, to which I have already made reference (see pp. 32–6, above), necrophilic elements are quite clearly to be found. Examples include sections on 'Sadistic lust murder' (*PS* 82–5), 'Anthropophagy' (*PS* 85–9), and 'Mutilation of corpses' (*PS* 90–5). It seems that only when it is isolated, and accorded its scientific name as a medico-legal category, can necrophilia strike such a chord of apparent revulsion in the sexologist.

This suggests, perhaps, the paradoxical power surrounding the act of naming. It is a commonplace that the act of naming something gives one dominion over it (God's gift to mankind of naming the things in the world; the husband's bestowing of his name upon his bride). Yet, there is plentiful evidence that the name, once given, can echo disturbingly in the ear of the bestower. Naming a frightening concept partially tames it, but simultaneously makes it present and real. The name begins to stand metonymically for the feared thing and may cause the same shock of recognition as the thing itself. A good example is the love that dare not speak its name, originally Victorian homosexuality, but equally applicable, perhaps, to necrophilia.

In the first of the *Three Essays on the Theory of Sexuality*, Freud openly acknowledges his debt to the sexologists, who fulfil the role of informative antecedents as well as an authority against which to argue. Freud's obvious innovation in this area lies in proposing a model of polymorphous sexuality as a universal stage of human development, and in his willingness to discuss such sexual taboos as incestuous desire in a non-moralizing tone. That said, consider Freud's attitude of wariness around the theorization of necrophilia:

> Nevertheless, in some of these perversions the quality of the new sexual aim is of a kind to demand special examination. Certain of them are so far removed from the normal in their content that we cannot avoid pronouncing them 'pathological'. This is especially so where (as, for instance, in cases of licking excrement or of intercourse with dead bodies) the sexual instinct goes to astonishing lengths in successfully overriding the resistances of shame, disgust, horror or pain. But even in such cases we should not be too ready to assume that people who act in this way will necessarily turn out to be insane or subject to grave abnormalities of other kinds. Here again we cannot escape from the fact that people whose behaviour is in other respects normal can, under the domination of the most unruly of all the instincts, put themselves in the category of sick persons in the single sphere of sexual life. (*SE* vii. 161)

The words 'pathological', 'disgust' and 'sick persons' make the tone of this passage from Freud hard to distinguish from that of the Krafft-Ebing extract on necrophilia. For two writers who aim to push forward the study of sexuality by open discussion of the perversions, the quoted passages reveal a surprising reserve. This is all the more surprising in the case of Freud, since, as I have examined above, the logic of his formulation of the death drive is to locate death at the heart of sexuality. That some should feel driven to act upon or to symbolize this in the world is perhaps not so surprising.

In order to see whether the more sexually repressed and repressive climate of the time could have influenced these coy accounts of necrophilia, I surveyed some late twentieth-century standard psychology and sociology texts and found striking similarities to the two *fin-de-siècle* theorists discussed above. A particularly telling rhetorical device was found in Kenneth Plummer's sociology text *Sexual Stigma* (1975). Plummer's aim is to demonstrate the socially constructed nature of sexual perversion. On four different occasions he uses necrophilia as the yardstick of extreme aberration. Two examples of this device are as follows: 'There is a world of difference between casual norm violation in bed between husband and wife consensually, and *a necrophiliac driven day after day to seek corpses, real or imaginary*, and organizing his life around this pursuit'[24] and 'All sexual experiences become socially organized. No matter what form sexuality takes—*from marital copulation through to necrophilic murder*—a social pattern is assumed.'[25] While Plummer's assertions may well be accurate, he misses, as a careful sociologist, the implicit meanings in the literariness of his own text. His rhetoric points unintentionally to an intrinsic paradox: necrophilia is present as the epitome of aberration, the extreme limit of experience. Yet its very extremity, the fact that he should so readily choose it for this role, implies that it is nonetheless a figure at the heart of perversion, endemic to it.

The most telling fact is that it is only in creating these comparative formulations that Plummer mentions necrophilia. There is no attempt anywhere in the book to theorize, explore or explain it. It is used only to signify the 'other' of 'comprehensible' sexual perversion. In this, it becomes a meta-perversion: it is that which lies one step removed from what can be explained. Thus, in many ways, necrophilia remains the 'Dark Continent' of perversion studies, the blind spot of theory. The tendency to mention it without supporting analysis or comment only adds to the mystification surrounding this concept.

What are we to make of this reluctance to admit necrophilic impulses as part of human nature? Regarding the contemporary reception of his work, Freud commented that, for scientists and public alike, his revelations concerning sexuality, particularly infantile sexuality, were met with a hostile unwillingness to accept. Freud interpreted this as a deep denial of what is most profound within us. Following Freud's own analysis then—that we refuse to see the things which are closest to us, which most threaten our sense of what we wish to be—we can deduce that Freud himself is reluctant to come to terms with the implications of the death–desire couple. In the early works, he is obsessed with sexuality. In the later works, we see what Laplanche describes as a *Zwang* towards auto-destructivity. Yet throughout, the manifestation of sexuality and death remains a textual *non-dit*.

In the first of Freud's *Three Essays on the Theory of Sexuality*, it is stated that the range and scope of sexual object-choice for the polymorphous infant is unlimited. It is only because of social demands for individual repression that what was once desired is shunned and becomes shameful or abhorrent:

Our study of the perversions has shown us that the sexual instinct has to struggle against certain mental forces which act as resistances, and of which shame and disgust are most prominent. It is permissible to suppose that these forces play a part in restraining that instinct within the limits that are regarded as normal; and if they develop in the individual before the sexual instinct has reached its full strength, it is no doubt that they will determine the course of its development.

[footnote, added 1915] On the other hand, these forces which act like dams upon sexual development—disgust, shame and morality—must also be regarded as historical precipitates of the external inhibitions to which the sexual instinct has been subjected during the psychogenesis of the human race. We can observe the way in which, in the development of individuals, they arise at the appropriate moment, as though spontaneously when upbringing and external influence give the signal. (*SE* vii. 162)

As in the sexual development of the social being, the history of theory seems to have bowed to the same forces of shame and disgust regarding the subject of necrophilia. This widespread silence means that there have been hardly any previous attempts to delineate a necrophilic imaginary.

Some Concluding Remarks

Freud's *Civilization and its Discontents* (1930) relies on the premiss that a selfish drive for sex and domination is the unmediated ambition of the subject. However, in the interests of self-preservation, the social being forgoes its acts of murder or rape and enters into a socio-psychical contract, demanding repression and sublimation of the antisocial and destructive impulses. Civilization is maintained at the expense of total individual freedom and the renunciation of libidinal pleasure. Freud's hydraulic model of the drives in *Beyond the Pleasure Principle* can be seen to describe the excess of this social compromise, that which escapes the neat containment of individual maverick desire. This desire for the beyond of pleasure may be turned into symptoms, or else be expressed in a sublimated and safe form in dreams and, of course, literature.

The preponderant expression of necrophilic sentiment in nine-teenth-century texts can be read as a culturally acceptable way of 'making safe' destructive impulses. This view is suggested by Marie Bonaparte, who writes of the necrophile Sergeant Bertrand, 'il faisait, en un mot, en grand, ce qu'Edgar Poe — l'inhibé — se contentait de rêver'.[26] I would perhaps not go so far as to suggest that the line between a necrophilic writer and a would-be practitioner is quite that thin, or that the equivalence between neurotic phantasy and acting out translates so literally and according to quite such a simple relation of cause and effect. Nonetheless, this idea supports the persuasive view that literature serves a social function by encoding, within a safe space, desires which must not be enacted in the world. However, the fear exists, as Krafft-Ebing has made clear, that such textual representation may simultaneously defuse and stimulate the impulse. This reaches the heart of contemporary debates on pornography, which question how far it is safe (and indeed helpful) to diffuse images and fantasies that facilitate sexual release, thereby possibly reducing the incidence of coercive sexual acts.[27]

In the case of necrophilic representations, a whole wealth of re- pressed sex- and death-related associations is evoked. The eroticized idealization of death, murder and the corpse in imaginative literature may function as a working through of ambivalent desirous and guilty impulses, seldom admitted to the surface of consciousness. Such writing stands as a permanent monument to desire, encrypted in words. Like the intra-psychic crypts described by Abraham and Török, which occur as a result of the failure of mourning, necrophilic writing is the failure to repress completely the destructive impulses. It is, to borrow Kristeva's terminology, the disruptive emergence of the Semiotic in the body of the Symbolic.[28]

Peter Brooks's seminal essay 'Freud's Masterplot' takes this idea onto another level. It suggests that the death drive is endemic to literature, visible not only in isolated eruptions of desire, but as the— tacit and unacknowledged—organizing principle of narrative. It is one of the few works of criticism to address the relationship between the death drive and creative form.[29]

Brooks posits that the very nature of literary storytelling is that it is fuelled by a desire for its own end: 'What operates in the text through repetition is the death instinct, the drive towards the end'[30] and 'Desire is the wish for the end, for fulfillment, but fulfillment must be delayed so that we can understand it in relation to its origin and to desire itself.'[31] He reads Freud's *Beyond the Pleasure Principle* as an exemplary tale of the relation between beginnings and endings. The desire to achieve a state of stasis is seen as the driving force that motivates the forward-flung desire of any text, as well as of any individual life. In suggesting that the death drive operates an intrinsically destructive creation, Brooks offers up literature as a privileged space where we may examine the workings of Thanatos, directing the course of sexuality into dying only in its own way.

The widespread idea that literature may enact the movements of desire is an important one for the continuing dynamic relationship between psychoanalysis and literature. Like Brooks's article, this book adds to that body of work which seeks to collapse the idea of the discursive authority of theory.[32] Psychoanalysis is not simply a tool with which to analyse literature; instead literature may serve to illustrate the gaps and silences on the part of psychoanalysis. It is profitable to read theory against itself, by holding it up to the scrutiny of a neighbouring discourse. In this way it may be possible to account for the repression and denial of what is implicitly present in the weft and warp of Freudian theory.

Notes to Chapter 2

1. Sigmund Freud, *Three Essays on the Theory of Sexuality*, Standard Edition [SE], vii. 125–245. All references to Freud's work are taken from *The Standard Edition of the Complete Psychological Works*, translated from the German under the general editorship of James Strachey, 24 vols. (London: Hogarth Press and Institute of Psycho-Analysis, 1953–74).

2. See especially Robert Stoller, *Perversion: The Erotic Form of Hatred* (Hassocks: Harvester, 1976), and M. Masud R. Khan, *Alienation in Perversions* (London: Hogarth Press and Institute of Psycho-Analysis, 1979). These works from the 1970s are informed by a conservative view of perversion as essentially aggressive and inhibitory to human love, intimacy and happiness. In *Creativity and Perversion* (London: Free Association Books, 1985), Janine Chasseguet-Smirgel similarly sees perversion as an antisocial and regressive phantasy mode, but also explores the creative dimensions of the (male) perverted imaginary. She casts the pervert in the role of transgressive rebel, rewriting Oedipal sexuality in the terms of the anal universe, in which generational and gender differences, and even the difference between life and death, may be disregarded. Joyce McDougall's *Plea for a Measure of Abnormality* (London: Free Association Books, 1990) is a forward-looking text which discusses the possibility of happiness and productivity for the subject whose erotic life falls outside heterosexual genitality. Louise Kaplan's *Female Perversions* (Harmondsworth: Penguin, 1991) is a feminist work which argues that such perversions as sadism, necrophilia and fetishism are uniquely male perversions. She locates female perversion in acts and fantasies of exaggerated passivity and self-harm (cutting, anorexia, unrequited sexual obsessions). Her thesis is, broadly, that if 'male' perversions can be understood as exaggerated stereotypes of masculinity, then 'female' perversions must be found in exaggerated embodiments of femininity. (She does not attempt to account for instances of female sadism, necrophilia and fetishism, which occur in reported clinical practice. I presume that she would assume such female subjects to be in the grip of a masculinity complex.) This brief overview of twentieth-century contributions to the field should give an idea of the major areas of debate that continue to preoccupy perversion theorists.

3. The exemplary French poem expressing the sentiment of *carpe diem* is Ronsard's 'A sa maistresse' (Ode XVII), *Œuvres complètes*, ed. Gustave Cohen, 3 vols., Pléiade (Paris: Gallimard, 1950), i. 419–20:

> Mignonne, allons voir si la rose
> Qui ce matin avait déclose

Sa robe de pourpre au soleil,
A point perdu, cette vêprée,
Les plis de sa robe pourpée
Et son teint au vôtre pareil.

4. For an ingenious exploration of the mechanisms and internal logic of Freud's essay and the concept of the death drive in the light of Lacanian theory, see Richard Boothby, *Death and Desire: Psychoanalytic Theory in Lacan's Return to Freud* (New York and London: Routledge, 1991).

5. However, see Hannah Segal, 'On the clinical usefulness of the concept of death instinct', *International Journal of Psychoanalysis* 74 (1993), 55–61. In this article Segal demonstrates convincingly that the death drive may be made manifest in dream condensations, slips of the tongue and sexual fantasies.

6. Jean Laplanche, *Vie et mort en psychanalyse* (Paris: Flammarion, 1970), 14.

7. Ibid., 185. This idea of the reflexive phase being the scene of internal conflict, later manifest as death drive, is interesting when compared with Lacan's idea of the entry of the human subject into language. This is the moment at which desire becomes expressible through words, which leads to a widening schism between speaking subject and object of desire that will never be bridged and that will lead to eternal frustration, sated only in death. Both are moments of profound internal division within and against the self.

8. Laplanche, *Vie et mort en psychanalyse*, 80.

9. Ibid., 188.

10. Leo Bersani, *Baudelaire and Freud* (Berkeley: University of California Press, 1977), 88.

11. According to Laplanche, *Vie et mort en psychanalyse*.

12. Albert Moll, *Handbuch der Sexualwissenschaften mit besonderer Berücksichtigung der kulturgeschichtlichen Bezierhungen* (Leipzig: F. C. W. Vogel, 1912).

13. The necrophilic killer John Christie gassed his later victims to the point of unconsciousness before strangling them and violating their corpses. He reported that his earlier victims' physical struggles for life had produced in him an anaphrodisiac effect (see Ludovic Kennedy, *10, Rillington Place* (London: Panther, 1971)).

14. Although I am arguing for the possibility of reading the myth at the most literal (and non-gendered) level here, important feminist work has been done on the symbol of the headless woman as a figure of fearful misogyny. Julia Kristeva's *Visions capitales* (Paris: Éditions de la Réunion des Musées Nationaux, 1998) explores the recurrent conceit in art and myth of decapitation, which is read as the radical splitting of the woman's mind from her body.

15. Ernest Jones, *On the Nightmare* (London: Hogarth Press and Institute of Psycho-Analysis, 1931).

16. Marie Bonaparte, *Edgar Poe: sa vie, son œuvre: étude analytique*, 3 vols. (Paris: Presses Universitaires de France, 1958), and 'Deuil, nécrophilie et sadisme à propos d'Edgar Poe', *Revue française de psychanalyse* 4 (1930–1), 716–34.

17. Gérard de Nerval, 'El Desdichado', *Œuvres complètes*, ed. Jean Guillaume and Claude Pichois, 3 vols., Pléiade (Paris: Gallimard, 1984–93), iii. 645.

18. Joseph S. Bierman, 'Necrophilia in a thirteen-year-old boy', *Psychoanalytic Quarterly* 31 (1962), 329–36.

19. Nicholas Abraham and Maria Török, *L'Écorce et le noyeau* (Paris: Flammarion, 1987), 261.
20. Ibid.
21. Serge Leclaire, *On tue un enfant* (Paris: Seuil, 1975).
22. Ibid., 13.
23. Ibid., 19.
24. Kenneth Plummer, *Sexual Stigma: an Interactionist Account* (London: Routledge and Kegan Paul, 1975), 72 (my italics).
25. Ibid., 85 (my italics). The other two examples of this rhetoric occur on p. 65 and p. 209.
26. Bonaparte, 'Deuil, nécrophilie et sadisme à propos d'Edgar Poe', 726.
27. The principal players in this debate are feminist theorists. The anti-pornography wing represented by Andrea Dworkin argues that pornographic images are always already misogynist and feed into the misogyny in our culture by reinforcing and encouraging the continuation of male sexual violence on women. Catharine MacKinnon claims that the offensive use of language in pornography translates directly into real action in the world. The counter-current is represented by such feminists as Gayle Rubin, Ellen Willis and Anne Snitow, who argue that censorship is more dangerous than free expression. For a thoughtful discussion of these questions and positions, see John Phillips, *Forbidden Fictions: Pornography and Censorship in Twentieth-Century French Literature* (London: Pluto Books, 1999), esp. 1–24.
28. For a discussion of the disruptive and revolutionary potential of artistic form, see Julia Kristeva, *La Révolution du langage poétique: l'avant-garde à la fin du XIXe siècle: Lautréamont et Mallarmé* (Paris: Seuil, 1974). For a discussion of desire in language, see Kristeva, *Polylogue* (Paris: Seuil, 1977).
29. See also Laura Mulvey's recent essay on the death drive and cinematic narrative, which is indebted to Brooks's essay: 'Death drives: Hitchcock's Psycho', *Film Studies* 2 (2000), 5–14.
30. Peter Brooks, 'Freud's masterplot', in *Reading for the Plot* (Oxford: Clarendon Press, 1984), 90–112 (102).
31. Ibid., 111.
32. For a seminal discussion of the interrelatedness of theory and literature, see Malcolm Bowie, *Freud, Proust, Lacan: Theory as Fiction* (Cambridge: Cambridge University Press, 1987).

CHAPTER 3

The Poetics of Baudelaire's *Liebestod*

> I wish we were dead together to-day,
> Lost sight of, hidden away out of sight,
> Clasped and clothed in the cloven clay,
> Out of the world's way, out of the light,
> Out of the ages of worldly weather,
> Forgotten of all men altogether,
> As the world's first dead, taken wholly away,
> Made one with death, filled full of the night.
>
> ALGERNON CHARLES SWINBURNE, 'The Triumph of Time'

Critical works devoted to Baudelaire tend to claim that his significance as a canonical figure of Western literature is due to his innovation in one of two fields. For commentators such as Albert Cassagne and Graham Chesters, Baudelaire is best remembered as a pioneer of poetics, experimenting with subject matter and prosody, giving birth to Symbolism, and developing the prose poem form. Philosophical and psychoanalytic critics, on the other hand, hold that Baudelaire's import lies in the fact that his writing constitutes a theoretical and aesthetic model of modern subjectivity. For such thinkers as Sartre and Bataille, Baudelaire's writing exemplifies key tensions in moral philosophy. For Walter Benjamin, it bears witness to the traumatic eclipsing of the pre-modern by the modern age. For the psychoanalytic critics Leo Bersani and René Laforgue, the poems exemplify the text-as-psyche, providing rich literary expressions of neurosis.

Several critics have pointed out the presence of subject matter relating to perverse sexual desire in Baudelaire's writing. In particular, much attention has been paid to Baudelaire's sadism, most visible in poems such as 'L'Héautontimorouménos', 'À celle qui est trop gaie' and 'À une Madone'.[1] So far, however, no study has foregrounded necrophilia as the imaginative paradigm which best characterizes Baudelaire's writing. Indeed Marie Bonaparte contends that whereas Poe is 'properly' necrophile, 'la nécrophilie, dans l'œuvre baude-lairien, disparaît sous le sadisme'.[2]

In *Baudelaire and Freud*, Leo Bersani discusses necrophilia as one aspect of Baudelaire's perverse persona. He introduces the concept of 'psychical mobility', to account for the movements of Baudelaire's phantasy trajectory from fetishistic desire for a head of hair ('La Chevelure') to sadism and masochism and to the necrophile figure of a worm devouring a corpse in 'Je t'adore à l'égal de la voûte nocturne'. For Bersani, both subject and object in Baudelaire are shifting, multiple, unformed and boundless. His short chapter 'Desire and death' uses a sample of Baudelaire's poetry and Freud's 'Economic problem in masochism' to illustrate some of the problems found when formulating a sexual excitement linked to the death drive. While his elucidation of death-driven desire is quite brilliant here,[3] the concept of necrophilia is underdeveloped. Bersani does not move beyond the Freudian model that sees death-driven perversion as having its logical outcome in sadism. He concludes that necrophilia is the result of a fear of sadomasochistic movement: 'The terror of motion in the ap-parently uncontrolled motions of sado-masochistic sexuality is betrayed—both in Baudelaire and Sade—by a fascination with corpses. Violating a dead body is a kind of immobile sex.'[4] This refusal to take into account the power of the positive attribute of deadness as a factor in arousing desire is typical of what we have seen in writing on the subject. Moreover, this echoes the stereotype of necrophilia, which holds that it is the cowardly or dull resort of a sort of sexual shyness, the underside of sadism. In my reading of Baudelaire's necrophilia below, I hope to show some of the ways in which necrophilia involves a radical fantasy of self-loss for the writer and mirrors his celebrated risk-taking at the artistic level. I shall suggest that necrophilia offers a convincing descriptive and dynamic model to account for Baudelaire's poetics and aesthetics, as well as his desiring poetic persona.

My reading of Baudelaire's necrophilia will contend that it is only by reconciling the two broad critical swaths of Baudelaire criticism (poetic and phenomenological) that one can fully appreciate both the poetry and the desire subtending it. Thus, Baudelaire's innovations in the field of poetry can be shown to be inextricably bound up with a particular desiring mode of subjectivity that has both universal and historical implications. I shall explore several strategies employed throughout Baudelaire's corpus which stage the necrophilic drama, including strategies of immobilization and transformation, structures of repetition, and a play between metaphorization and de-metaphorization, which can be read as operating on both the literary and the psychical level.

Death Drives in Baudelaire's Poetry

Les Fleurs du Mal provides ample evidence that Baudelaire is a writer obsessed with death. In numerous poems, particularly those in the section entitled 'La Mort', Baudelaire seeks death as the desired end to the pain and ennui of life. In 'La Fin de la journée', the poet shuns life, described as 'impudente et criarde' and welcomes the comforting arms of death:

> Le Poète se dit: 'Enfin!
>
> Mon esprit, comme mes vertèbres,
> Invoque ardemment le repos;
> Le cœur plein de songes funèbres,
>
> Je vais me coucher sur le dos
> Et me rouler dans vos rideaux,
> Ô rafraîchissantes ténèbres!'
> (*OC* i. 128)

Wanting to die, then, is somehow safe for Baudelaire in these writings. Death represents the ultimate succour of oblivion, dressed in the guise of a long sleep. However, the adverb 'ardemment', usually suggesting a burning passion, and the use of the oxymoronic 'rafraîchissantes ténèbres' injects a note of concupiscence into the picture. If death promises sleep, then the sleep is at least potentially exciting.

In the well-known closing lines of 'Le Voyage', this tension is more fully drawn. Life is unchallenging and predictable, while Death is the exciting, enlivening alternative. It is presented as a Mallarméen dice throw *avant la lettre*, its outcome uncertain. Its contemplation provides a thrill of desire:

> Ô Mort, vieux capitaine, il est temps! levons l'ancre!
> Ce pays nous ennuie, ô Mort! Appareillons!
> Si le ciel et la mer sont noirs comme de l'encre,
> Nos cœurs que tu connais sont remplis de rayons!

Verse-nous ton poison pour qu'il nous réconforte!
Nous voulons, tant ce feu nous brûle le cerveau,
Plonger au fond du gouffre, Enfer ou Ciel, qu'importe?
Au fond de l'inconnu pour trouver du *nouveau*! (*OC* i. 134)

It has been usual to read these lines as a statement of Baudelaire's continuing belief in the religious concept of an afterlife, despite his formulations elsewhere suggesting that death leads only to sleep. Whether heaven or hell will receive him, going somewhere through death seems in this poem better than the state of stasis that life—paradoxically—suggests. Baudelaire consciously perceives the tension between the pleasures of the calm and harmonious and the desire for disruption and destruction to exist in the human subject, seen when he writes of those human actions which 'n'ont d'attrait que *parce que* elles sont mauvaises, dangereuses; elles possèdent l'attirance du gouffre' (*OC* ii. 322).

Sartre emphasizes this aspect of Baudelaire's writing, pointing out that the Satanist, unlike the athiest, retains a keen awareness of the presence of God whom he hates rather than negates. (For example, in 'Abel et Caïn', 'Race de Caïn, au ciel monte / Et sur la terre jette Dieu!' is a challenge to God rather than an assertion that God is dead.) For Sartre, the essence of Baudelairean 'evil' lies in the consciousness of wrongdoing.

Sartre states: 'Faire le Mal pour le Mal, c'est très exactement faire tout exprès le contraire de ce que l'on continue d'affirmer comme le Bien. C'est vouloir ce qu'on ne veut pas—puisque le Bien se définit toujours comme l'objet et la fin de la volonté profonde.'[5] I would like to cast a Freudian spin on this formula of evil as the deliberate move to want that which cannot be wanted. In the terms of the discourse of Christianity, suicide is a sin because only God—that is, a being other than and greater than the self—can give death. The death drive provides a secular model of this paradigm of lawbreaking. The life-driven pleasure principle is a model of calm and ease that the death-driven subject seeks to exceed.

In one rather odd poem in 'La Mort', 'Le Rêve d'un curieux', the poetic voice recounts a dream of his own death:

J'étais comme l'enfant avide du spectacle,
Haïssant le rideau comme on hait un obstacle ...
Enfin la vérité froide se révéla:

J'étais mort sans surprise, et la terrible aurore
M'enveloppait. — Eh quoi! n'est-ce donc que cela?
La toile était levée et j'attendais encore. (*OC* i. 129)

The poem is dedicated to a friend of Baudelaire's, Félix Nadar, known for his vociferous atheism.[6] On one level, then, the message of the dream is a confirmation of Nadar's position: the afterlife is a myth and nothing waits for our souls after death. On the other hand, the poem reveals a strange sense of personal disappointment. Poetic suspense is created by use of the *points de suspension* and the revelatory 'enfin', building up the reader's expectation in the last line of the first tercet. However, a bathetic note is then struck in the last stanza with 'n'est-ce donc que cela?' and the poem ends with the words 'et j'attendais encore.'

We are reminded of Freud's odd contention in *Beyond the Pleasure Principle* that the death drive describes the organism's wish to die only in its own way. Death itself is revealed as a disappointment in 'Le Rêve d'un curieux'. This suggests that the 'sleep' itself is less interesting to Baudelaire than the manner in which it happens, the transformative moment of falling. The title of 'Le Voyage', the last poem in the collection, is telling. Approaching death involves an odyssey, a projection. Desire is maintained not by achieving the goal, but by projecting oneself, imaginatively, into the non-return of the future. I would disagree with Sartre's assertion that Baudelaire is haunted by an imperfect and unalterable past and that he writes from the point of view of one looking back at life from the vantage point of death. When Baudelaire steps too far into an unknowable space, as in 'Le Rêve d'un curieux', bathos is the inevitable outcome: the poem enacts a logical tautology. The only way desire can function is in forward motion, even if, paradoxically, the drive under which desire is operating is for a return to the inorganic.

The difficulty of formulating the knots and contradictions in logic revealed in both Freud's writing on the death drive and Baudelaire's poetry comes in the recognition that these are attempts to describe the ineffable. What these poems reveal is a series of psychological attitudes towards, and fantasies of, death. They are never about death itself but always about a mediated relation to it, for that is all that can be expressed.

The 'quiet sleep' is juxtaposed with a second sort of dying, involving a vertiginous drop. This is hinted at in the closing lines of 'Le Voyage', where the removal of tension can come only after tension has first been increased. I would suggest that this second idea of death is the aspect to which Baudelaire is most attracted. Baudelaire's fantasy is the bliss of easeful death, excitingly delivered. The avowed overthrowal of God and the fantasy of narrating one's own death are equally attempts to invert hierarchy and assert individual creative will.

In her study of the creative nature of the perversions, Janine Chasseguet-Smirgel writes: 'The pervert is trying to free himself from the paternal universe and the constraints of the law. He wants to create a new kind of reality and to dethrone God the Father.'[7] For Chasseguet-Smirgel, perversion results from an infantile refusal to accept the barriers against incestuous and cross-generational sexuality. This leads to a collapsing within the adult psyche of the acceptable and unacceptable zones of pleasure, including the barriers of life and death. 'God the Father' here is a projection of the father as god, and, by extension, of the patriarchal social order. Death-driven perversion in Baudelaire can be read as both an intensely narcissistic and a radically antisocial force. Baudelaire's poetry can be seen as a restless series of attempts to thematize and embody the ideal approach to death.

Modes of Necrophilia in Baudelaire's Poetry

While I have argued above that Baudelaire's death wish can be read as a solipsistic figure pointing to a rejection of life and society, Baudelaire does not always figure death as something that one does alone. Indeed, the lonely disappointment seen at the end of 'Le Rêve d'un curieux' seems to come almost from the unexpected emptiness of the abyss. In many of the *Fleurs du Mal*, Baudelaire celebrates the idea of the other's death or of dying together. This idea is conveyed sometimes by means of poetic devices suggesting allegorical or metaphorical necrophilia, sometimes by a celebration of murder and contemplation of the idealized corpse.

Allegorical necrophilia

In certain poems, most obviously 'Je t'adore à l'égal de la voûte nocturne', the poet imagines that the female lover he describes is a corpse. The poem opens with metaphorical descriptions of the woman that suggest coldness and frigidity ('vase de tristesse', 'grande taciturne'). These become progressively more extreme until the climax of the poem:

> Je m'avance à l'attaque, et je grimpe aux assauts,
> Comme après un cadavre un chœur de vermisseaux,

> Et je chéris, ô bête implacable et cruelle!
> Jusqu'à cette froideur par où tu m'es plus belle! (*OC* i. 27)

In these final lines, her figurative (sexual) coldness becomes the rigor of death and his violent exertion on her passive body is likened to worms devouring a corpse.

At first one may think that necrophilia is at most a figurative device in this poem. The corpse is evoked as a vicious attack on some unfortunate former mistress or in the interests of bad taste—to *épater les bourgeois*. However, it is important to remember that nothing in poetry is ever merely a figure: figurative language is the substance of poetry itself, the heart of the poetic. Secondly, the theme and the devices used in the poem suggest a more pervasive obsessive quality, as we will see them repeated and modified in other poems.

The dynamic suggested above is one of equivalence. The concepts of death and sexuality are associatively linked by simile, the device of choice for expressing the conjunction of two ideas in the service of poetic charge and artistic renewal. However, it may also suggest an unconscious process. Following Jakobson and Halle's *Fundamentals of Language* (1956), metaphor has been linked to the psychical operation of condensation, and metonymy to displacement. Simile can be seen as closer to metaphor, as it is signifies similarity, rather than contiguity.[8]

Simile and other poetic devices for comparing terms also suggest simultaneity. Unlike metaphor, where the thing described is absent, silenced, and another signifier stands in its place, simile keeps the two terms in play, so that each suggests and cancels out the other equally. Consider the following lines from 'Hymne à la beauté':

> L'amoureux pantelant incliné sur sa belle
> A l'air d'un moribond caressant son tombeau. (*OC* i. 25)

'A l'air de' works like 'comme' to suggest an immediate conjunction between the two key ideas across the lines. Simultaneous meaning can be conveyed in poetry, as reading is not merely forward-driven and chronological. Words, sounds and meanings are triggered retro-actively, echoing back through rhyme, rhythmic patterning and assonance. Here, the unexpected image of death nuances the meaning of the previous lines, as 'beau'—the final syllable of 'tombeau'—provides an apt and ironic complement to 'belle'. The simile, and the way in which we read it, presents the perfect device for embodying the paradoxical drive of Thanatos, which is both propelled by desire and compelled to repeat foundational structures and patterns.

The 'comme' of the simile may also suggest the psychical mechanism of identification. In 'Une nuit que j'étais près d'une affreuse juive', the poet describes his supine position beside the unattractive prostitute as 'Comme au long d'un cadavre, un cadavre étendu'. The simile collapses the subject and object of the poem into the figure of the corpse. Also, the poetic device of chiasmus, a profound phonic echoing at the heart of a line of verse, is particularly apt here in helping to suggest a *mise en abyme* of deathliness. The figure of the corpse, with which the poet associates both object and self, is repeated in the structure of the line, suggesting both sameness and mirroring, identification and a reluctant, ambivalent desire.

Some of the most original uses of the simile to link sexuality and death are found in 'Une charogne'. The poem takes the form of an address by the poet to his mistress. He reminds her of the time they encountered a putrid animal carcass on a walk in the countryside, leading him to meditate on her mortality.

The description of the carcass is powerful:

> Les jambes en l'air, comme une femme lubrique,
>   Brûlante et suant les poisons,
> Ouvrait d'une façon nonchalante et cynique
>   Son ventre plein d'exhalaisons. (*OC* i. 31)

Sexuality and death are united by use of the simile in a crude parody of female sexual receptiveness. The excretions ('poisons', 'exhalaisons') evoke the corporeal emissions suggested both by sexual excitement and death. Where *carpe diem* poems traditionally use images of fading flowers euphemistically to suggest the corpse, Baudelaire names the thing in the most explicit terms possible. Indeed, rather than implying that fading flowers are like decaying matter, Baudelaire deliberately inverts this order in his extraordinary formulation 'Et le ciel regardait la carcasse superbe / comme une fleur s'épanouir'.

The poem is deliberately perverse, as Baudelaire uses these techniques to mock and challenge accepted mores—here the reverence with which one is accustomed to treat the subject of impending death. The nineteenth-century Romantic movement saw the inception of a general preoccupation with the question of what was and was not fit subject matter for poetic art. Baudelaire and his contemporaries clearly saw it as their role to continue to enlarge the field of lexical and thematic opportunity by making nameable that which had previously been taboo, and mixing high and low registers of language to create new effects.[9]

In its treatment of the physical realities of decomposition, 'Une charogne' is unparalleled:

> Les mouches bourdonnaient sur ce ventre putride,
> D'où sortaient de noirs bataillons
> De larves, qui coulaient comme un épais liquide
> 20   Le long de ces vivants haillons.
>
> Tout cela descendait, montait comme une vague,
> Ou s'élançait en pétillant;
> On eût dit que le corps, enflé d'un souffle vague,
> 24   Vivait en se multipliant.
>
> Et ce monde rendait une étrange musique,
> Comme l'eau courante et le vent,
> Ou le grain qu'un vanneur d'un mouvement rythmique
> 28   Agite et tourne dans son van. (*OC* i. 31)

Where we would perhaps most expect unrelieved images of stillness, in the description of the dead matter, Baudelaire gives us a symphony of noise, movement and chaos. The images of bees, streams of liquid larvae, the sea, wind and winnowing create a mass of synaesthetic impressions, most of which would normally be likened to life rather than death. The alliteration of 'v' and 'm' in the stanzas, as seen in 'mouche', 'ventre', 'vivants', 'montait', 'vague', 'vague', 'vivait', 'multipliant', 'monde', 'musique', is also telling. *La vie* and *la mort* are being suggested, juxtaposed and mingled by the use of words which have the same initial letters. The poem enacts by its very form the morbid eagerness with which the recollected scenario is being reconstructed and relived.

At the end of the poem, closure is achieved by bringing the chaotic force of death back into the realm of the poet's control: he projects the energy generated by the fantasy onto his mistress in the form of a thinly disguised wish for her demise:

> — Et pourtant vous serez semblable à cette ordure,
> À cette horrible infection,
> Étoile de mes yeux, soleil de ma nature,
> Vous, mon ange et ma passion!

> Oui! telle vous serez, ô la reine des grâces (*OC* i. 32)

His living mistress and the carcass are made into equivalent terms following the logic of the poem. This is emphasized by the presence of two formulae to suggest equivalence ('vous serez semblable', 'telle vous serez'), which echo repetitively. This poem attempts both to pervert and to demystify the convention it plays with. It makes literal the hidden impulses subtending the memento mori and makes manifest the very stuff of death and decay.

Necrophilic murder

It is easy to see why critics have focused on the predominance of sadism in poems which enact the murder of a woman, such as 'À celle qui est trop gaie' or 'À une Madone'. However, such readings ignore the ideational centrality of death in these works.

'À celle qui est trop gaie' embodies the imaginative psychical journey towards a fantasy of shared death. It opens by describing a woman whose liveliness and verve touch and astonish those around her:

> Ta tête, ton geste, ton air
> Sont beaux comme un beau paysage;
> Le rire joue en ton visage
> Comme un vent frais dans un ciel clair. (*OC* i. 156)

An impression of beauty and harmony is created by the profusion of 'natural' images and the sing-song rhythms of the first three stanzas. This is succeeded by an abrupt break in tone and rhythm, as the poet moves to describe his own emotional landscape:

> Quelquefois dans un beau jardin
> Où je traînais mon atonie,
> J'ai senti, comme une ironie,
> Le soleil déchirer mon sein;
>
> Et le printemps et la verdure
> Ont tant humilié mon cœur,
> Que j'ai puni sur une fleur
> L'insolence de la Nature. (*OC* i. 157)

The discord between beauty, light and life, and the 'atonie' he feels leads to the embittered and lifeless poet destroying a flower in a symbolic attempt to reduce life to death. This becomes the extended metaphor that he imports to the heart of the relationship with the woman.

The rest of the poem takes the form of a fantasy of sexual death. In contrast to the sunlit brightness of the poem's opening, we now move into an interior space, suggesting both the bedchamber and the poet's libidinal fantasy realm:

> Ainsi je voudrais, une nuit,
> Quand l'heure des voluptés sonne,

> Vers les trésors de ta personne,
> Comme un lâche, ramper sans bruit (*OC* i. 157)

The ambience of crime is set up in the stanza, given by the atmospheric evocation of midnight 'l'heure des voluptés', intimations of hidden loot 'les trésors de ta personne' and stealthiness 'ramper sans bruit'. The resonant rhyming of 'personne' and 'sonne' creates a heavy resonant echo at the ends of the two lines.

The attack comes in the following stanza:

> Pour châtier ta chair joyeuse,
> Pour meurtrir ton sein pardonné,
> Et faire à ton flanc étonné
> Une blessure large et creuse,
>
> Et, vertigineuse douceur!
> À travers ces lèvres nouvelles,
> Plus éclatantes et plus belles,
> T'infuser mon venin, ma sœur! (*OC* i. 157)

An impression of mounting desire is created by the repetition of 'pour' at the beginning of the lines. 'Pour' suggests inexorable purpose, a dash towards a final aim. The terms of the attack are very special. In his discussion of this poem, Leo Bersani suggests that 'the crime involves nothing less than a re-creation of sexuality' and that the lips created by the poet's wounding 'are there in order to change sex into murder'.[10] In fact, the simile is absent this time: we are no longer focusing on the proximity of sex and murder or of life and death. Instead, there is no longer sex; there is only murder. The wounding both suggests an act of creation, something innovative and new, and also evokes a return to something originary, a reunion between the poet and his 'sœur'.

This is a poem about the elimination of differences. The poet tells us from the beginning what separates him from his love object: she belongs to the pole of life; he to the pole of death. The increasing frustration in the mismatch between them points to a tension both desirous and unbearable. The second half of the poem focuses on the way in which he contrives poetically and imaginatively to transform the dialectic of life and death and to create equivalence between them. While the mentions of punishment throughout the poem, and the frenzy visible in the lead-up to the attack ('vertigineuse douceur'), may suggest sadism, the necrophilic ambition of the poem is foregrounded in the closing image: the mistress is reborn in death as his sister. The familial bond is used to suggest sameness: she is remade in the image of how he feels himself to be. Thus, the poet actualizes his death-driven ambitions on the other.

In 'À une Madone', a fantasized religious icon, a statue of Mary, is animated by the poetic imagination and finally killed by seven knives, representing the seven sins. Here, Baudelaire plays consciously with sacrilegious images to debunk religious authority. One technique the poem employs is to name and enumerate the decorative objects that adorn the Madonna. These are then collapsed onto ideas and emotions:

> Je ferai pour ta tête une énorme Couronne,
> Et dans ma Jalousie, ô mortelle Madone,
> Je saurai te tailler un Manteau, de façon
> Barbare, roide et lourd ... (*OC* i. 58)

In this way the poem creates a blasphemous rosary in words, a set of signifiers that symbolically evoke something 'beyond' the material. The poetic *enjeu* can be seen to show up the hypocritical cherishing of objects and images in the supposedly spiritual discourse of religion. Moreover, it hints at the violence and desire subtending much apparently devout iconography.

The insistent focus on inanimate objects throughout the poem contrasts with the fluid, frenzied urgency of the killing in the final lines:

> Je les planterai tous dans ton Cœur pantelant,
> Dans ton Cœur sanglotant, dans ton Cœur ruisselant! (*OC* i. 59)

The hissing susurration of 'sanglotant' and 'ruisselant' is an effective device for embodying the gushing forth of blood from the body. Where previously the poem has adopted very regular alexandrine lines, in these two lines the caesura is decentred, suggesting a destruction of formal regularity. The poem plays with structures of mobility and immobility, at first animating a statue, decorating her, then killing her, and, finally, focusing on the flow of blood as it pours from the wounds. The unsettling motions of life and its idealized counterpart death are alternated with increasing rapidity in the attempt to cancel out the difference between them.

There may be a temptation to read the two poems discussed above as describing displaced and transformed sadistic orgasms, gained by killing rather than sex. However, it is my contention that orgasm—or any high point of tension and release—is a mere hiatus in the terms of poetic economy being described. It is death itself, not the 'little death', that is being sought.

Necrophilic voyeurism: 'Une martyre'

'Une martyre' treats of the reactions of a viewer standing before an unknown painting depicting a murdered woman. Few critics choose to talk about this poem in any depth. Georges Blin, who makes fleeting mention of it, remarks upon the strangeness of the fact that this poem was not banned along with the other condemned pieces: 'ce poème [...] excède les bornes de l'odieux. [...] Baudelaire y a mis l'accent d'une façon *insupportable* sur le côté charnel de la scène'.[11] My reading of 'Une martyre' will pose the question why Baudelaire's treatment of the scenario should seem 'insupportable' to a reader. It will propose a different reason from the one given by Blin, couched as it is in the rhetoric of good taste and moral disapproval.

The poem is a complex one, structured around several imaginative leaps. These include slippage between signifiers of time and place, and a series of shifting identifications between the poetic persona and the objects evoked. The opening stanza is in the form of a rather baroque description of the room depicted in the painting, characterized by an enumeration of decorative objects and polished surfaces:

> Au milieu des flacons, des étoffes lamées
> Et des meubles voluptueux,
> Des marbres, des tableaux, des robes parfumées
> Qui traînent à plis somptueux,
>
> Dans une chambre tiède où, comme en une serre,
> L'air est dangereux et fatal,
> Où des bouquets mourants dans leurs cercueils de verre
> Exhalent leur soupir final (*OC* i. 111–12)

An oppressive atmosphere of confinement is created. The imaginative space of the poem is a *chambre close*, which itself is captured within the frame of the picture at which the poet gazes. The first organic signifiers in the poem—flowers—are not only succumbing to necrosis, but are constrained by the glass vases, which serve as their 'cercueil'. The animate is framed by the inanimate. This is seen also in the choice of rhyme words: the suffocating 'serre' and the icy 'verre' create contradictory, but equally effective, images of entrapment.

The mention of the flowers falling into death is, as I have stated above, a traditional poetic symbol for impending mortality. Here it is used to announce the object of our interest:

> Un cadavre sans tête épanche, comme un fleuve,
>   Sur l'oreiller désaltéré
> Un sang rouge et vivant, dont la toile s'abreuve
>   Avec l'avidité d'un pré. (*OC* i. 112)

The headless corpse has an intriguing relation to stillness and mobility. On the one hand, it is 'just' another inanimate object, alongside the 'flacons', 'étoffes lamées' and 'marbres' of the opening lines. Yet the stream of blood, which flows like a river, suggests a new movement, which makes the decapitated head potentially relive in an altered form. As we have seen in 'Une charogne', immobility allows for a reanimation on a different level.

The splitting of the object into animate flow of blood/inanimate body is intensified by the division of head and body that occurs. While the body with its vivid, viscous flush of red symbolizes a form of ongoing vitality, the head is 'semblable aux visions pâles qu'enfante l'ombre'; it has slipped into a total inanimate state. In the fifth verse, material objects are prioritized. The head is situated 'sur la table de nuit'. The familiarity of this banal piece of bedroom furniture presents a sharp and shocking contrast with the vacuous gaze—'le regard vague et blanc'—of the murdered head.

The poet's focus then returns to the body, which is 'nu' and is stretched out in a fashion suggesting abandonment or sexual rapture. The corpse is eroticized by means of a fetishistic focus on certain talismanic parts and accessories:

> Un bas rosâtre, orné de coins d'or, à la jambe,
>   Comme un souvenir est resté;
> La jarretière, ainsi qu'un œil secret qui flambe,
>   Darde un regard diamanté. (*OC* i. 112)

Mention of her garter serves as a grotesque posthumous coquetry, while her inanimate leg is linked, through rhyme, with the burning flame of the passionate gaze. This suggests the constant revivification of the martyred body through the secret, silent, watching male gaze. The fixing of the female body and the splitting of the body into part objects are recognizable as the dynamic of fetishism. However, the fact that the object is a corpse, relic in the world of the unknowable realm of death, means that the possibility of complete appropriation and reification is suspended.

The poem takes these contrasting motifs of possession and excess a step further as spectacle shades into speculation:

> Le singulier aspect de cette solitude
> Et d'un grand portrait langoureux,
> Aux yeux provocateurs comme son attitude,
> Révèle un amour ténébreux,
>
> Une coupable joie et des fêtes étranges
> Pleines de baisers infernaux,
> Dont se réjouissait l'essaim des mauvais anges
> Nageant dans les plis des rideaux (*OC* i. 112)

The poet imagines the bizarre sexual encounter which led to the killing. Where the fetishist savours the object itself, little wishing to be reminded of what mother does not have, the necrophile is in search of the origins of desire. He probes and prods at the surface image of the corpse, eager to discover the secret hidden beneath this icon of death in life, the proof that one can die.

The poem then embarks on a reconstruction of the stages that led to the murder. Consider stanzas 11, 12 and 13:

> Elle est bien jeune encor! — Son âme exaspérée
> Et ses sens par l'ennui mordus
> S'étaient-ils entr'ouverts à la meute altérée
> Des désirs errants et perdus?
>
> L'homme vindicatif que tu n'as pu, vivante,
> Malgré tant d'amour, assouvir,
> Combla-t-il sur ta chair inerte et complaisante
> L'immensité de son désir?
>
> Réponds, cadavre impur! et par tes tresses roides
> Te soulevant d'un bras fiévreux,
> Dis-moi, tête effrayante, a-t-il sur tes dents froides
> Collé les suprêmes adieux? (*OC* i. 113)

The sudden, explosive 'Elle est bien jeune encor!' causes the corpse to come alive again momentarily. This is suggested by the attribution of her gender in the personal pronoun and the direct address to her as 'tu'. We are also presented with the shadowy figure of the absent lover and killer. The address to the dead woman as 'tu' suggests a strong wishful identification on the part of the poet with 'l'homme vindicatif'.

The urgency of the imperatives 'Réponds, cadavre impur!' and 'Dis-moi, tête effrayante' suggests the mounting excitement caused by the imaginative foray into the scene. However, frustration is revealed by the question mark at the end of each stanza, as the answer to the riddle of death and desire remains beyond the poet's grasp. The dead object will not revive sufficiently to answer him. These question marks signal the *élément limite* of the scenario. No more can be known; but desire, as speculation, may run on.

Something approaching resignation on the part of the poetic voice characterizes stanza 14:

> — Loin du monde railleur, loin de la foule impure,
>   Loin des magistrats curieux,
> Dors en paix, dors en paix, étrange créature,
>   Dans ton tombeau mystérieux (*OC* i. 113)

Having exhausted the possibilities of the scene for a mere onlooker, he urges the reawakened phantoms of desire back to sleep. The soothing repetition of 'Dors en paix, dors en paix' and the alliterative and sonorous echo of 'Dans ton tombeau mystérieux' reinforce the idea of the profundity and enigma of death for its beholder.

The final stanza takes a step outside the room in the picture and focuses on the absent, imagined figure of the killer, who inhabits the world beyond the scene:

> Ton époux court le monde, et ta forme immortelle
>   Veille près de lui quand il dort;
> Autant que toi sans doute il te sera fidèle,
>   Et constant jusques à la mort. (*OC* i. 113)

Here the killer has become 'ton époux', suggesting that their celebration of desire and death has married the couple in some eternal union. Moreover, the differences between agent and victim are blurred: she will be the active presence who 'Veille près de lui quand il dort', he the inanimate sleeper.

The imaginative trip through time, the impossibility of opening up the life–death divide, and the complex process of identification that form the last section give a telling account of the structural nature of fantasy. The poetic voice attempts to identify with the corpse. However, because of its nature—radical absence—familiarity and comprehension are impossible. The next-best identification is with the murderer, he who has experienced her death. The poet reanimates the corpse in order to kill her again, to undergo, through a shifting identification with killer and victim, the moment of death. The theme of decapitation in the poem has particular resonance. The question of who can and cannot see is an important one here. We cannot help but think of the uncanny cameo of the Medusa's head as we behold the 'tête effrayante'. However, following my argument in the previous chapter, I contend that the head in question here is not so much an icon of castration as one of radical annihilation. When the poet futilely exhorts the corpse to speak, it is to reveal the mysteries, not of female sexuality, but of death—specifically, the secret of her own death. Her blank gaze and her silence certainly represent disenfranchisement. However, we are not dealing primarily with the social subordination of the 'castrated' female, but with the horror and absolute stillness of murder.

'Une martyre' is a meditation on seeing death. The poem is constructed like a theatrical spectacle, with several voyeurs present. For the twenty-first-century reader, it may also suggest a cinematic quality. Death and sexuality on screen are the subject matter of choice of both Hollywood and art-house films. We may understand this phenomenon in light of that feature of psychical life which is the impossibility of outliving—much less viewing retroactively—one's own death. Death is only ever experienced in life when it is visible to us. The tableau described by Baudelaire exercises a hypnotic effect on the watcher, a result of simultaneous proximity to and distance from the scene. It encourages the watcher—and, by extension, the identifying reader—to make meaningful connections between the disparate objects presented. This phenomenon is similar to what is meant in cinematic theory by 'suture'.

We have seen how the *mise en scène* of the poem is reminiscent of a crime scene, enhanced by the very visual quality of Baudelaire's descriptions of objects and body parts. We focus on one and then another, just as if a camera were moving over them. Baudelaire's mobilizing and immobilizing strokes of the pen achieve in language what Hitchcock would later achieve cinematographically in his famous editing of the *Psycho* shower scene, where frenzied shots of the stabbing are followed by a still close-up of Janet Leigh's 'dead' face.

Georges Blin thought 'Une martyre' to be 'insupportable' because of the prurience he espied in Baudelaire's treatment of sexual murder. It is certainly true that this poem is not easy to read and makes a strong impact on the reader. However, the strong reaction the poem evokes is a result, I would suggest, not of the ghoulish subject matter *tout court*, but of the perfect embodiment of a structure of desire in appropriate and striking poetic form. The voyeurism allowed for in the poem positions the reader uncomfortably alongside the desiring poet and calls her/his own desire into question. For us as contemporary readers, saturated with the voyeurism of multimedia culture, 'Une martyre' provides a prophetically resonant insight into our own vicarious enjoyment of spectacles of sexuality and death that are as compulsive as they are disturbing.

Post-Mortem

In these poems, ideas of murder and love are collapsed onto each other, such that love scenes mutate into crime scenes and back again. Baudelaire's metaphorical description of love as 'un crime (où l'on ne peut pas se passer d'un complice)' (*OC* i. 689) is not an isolated or incidental one. Murder is not a metaphor for sex. Rather, murder is idealized and prioritized in such a way that it wholly replaces sex.

The described collaboration of killer and victim is one of the most troubling aspects of these poems. In 'Une martyre' and the murder poems, the described female object is in each case implicated in the drama as a partner as well as a victim. The necessary factor in the love–death play is the very complicity that the victims/lovers have to feel.[12] This would suggest that Baudelaire wants to go beyond murder as a mere literary figure and instead finds therein the structural formula for a relation or imagined relation of desire that is as violent as it is irresistibly seductive.

This dynamic is explored elsewhere in nineteenth-century poetry. In 'Porphyria's Lover', a poem by Baudelaire's English contemporary Browning, an adulterous lover strangles his married mistress with her own hair, so that they may remain together:

> That moment she was mine, mine fair
> Perfectly pure and good: I found
> A thing to do, and all her hair
> In one long yellow string I wound
> Three times her little throat around
> And strangled her. No pain felt she,
> I am quite sure she felt no pain.

In the closing lines, we see again the suggestion that the victim is a consenting party to the crime. This is given in the narrator's insistence upon the fulfilment of her 'wish' to remain with him:

> Porphyria's love: she guessed not how
> Her darling one wish would be heard.
> And thus we sit together now,
> And all night long we have not stirred,
> And yet God has not said a word![13]

Although this poem may be read as a ghoulish example of the way in which dominant masculine desire objectifies and projects onto the woman, it can be seen equally to reveal something about the way in which desire functions in the necrophile economy. The victim has to be seen to be both satisfied by her death and in an enviable position. Wishful identification is the mechanism by which the killer relates to the victim.

This structure would support my suggestion that the real subject and object of the deathly drama is the subject (poet) himself, and that the beloved is an internalized, highly idealized object that forms part of the poet's psyche and with which there is strong identification. Thus, the woman's identity is borrowed to allow the game to be played: the poet is doing to her (the part of him that is split off as an other) what he cannot do to himself. The idea of being, simultaneously, the one who ends life and the one whose life is ended is a thematic obsession which runs through Baudelaire's writing. In his 'Notes nouvelles sur Edgar Poe', he writes of man's 'perversité naturelle, qui fait que l'homme est sans cesse et à la fois homicide et suicide, assassin et bourreau' (*OC* ii. 323), and, in 'Mon cœur mis à nu', he avers: 'Il serait peut-être doux d'être alternativement victime et bourreau' (*OC* i. 676).

The poetic actualization of the desire for death is logically a tautology in that it, at the same time, announces the foreclosure of desire. If the poet remains to address his objects, the orgasm of un-creation is not one of absolute finality. The very violence of the description and its creative power forestall the trip into nothingness. The poetic objects, and finally the poem itself, are stilled at their end, but the poet's voice must live on to play out its destructive fantasy in further forms. This is disappointing, as the true desired outcome of the necrophile's encounter is that it should lead also to his death. Perhaps Baudelaire comes close to expressing this frustrating tension by writing the conflictual moments of desire into the syntactic and poetic substance of the work with its gaps, hesitations and jumps.

Cannibalizing Delacroix: Baudelaire and *La Madeleine dans le désert*

An obvious deduction following the argument of this chapter so far would be that art which is about murder idealized as love is the libidinal equivalent of transforming horror into pleasure on an artistic level. Much of Baudelaire's writing on other artists and writers concentrates on his conception of the conscious project of art, the transforming of ugliness into beauty: 'C'est un des privilèges prodigieux de l'Art que l'horrible, artistiquement exprimé, devienne beauté' (*OC* ii. 123). This desire to tame horror, to make it palatable, while elevating the figure of the artist to the status of a god, is rather like the technique of dressing murder as consensual sexuality: the thrill is experienced while the original sense of the abyss is turned aside. Baudelaire has much to say about this notion of idealizing transformation, not least in his critical response to contemporary art.

Baudelaire's transcendental view of art can help to explain his admiration for Delacroix, the painter whose images of carnage and riotous destruction, and interplay of the immobile and the fluid, so resemble Baudelaire's own poetic landscape. Indeed, in a critique of Meissanier's drawing *La Barricade*, Delacroix wrote, in words that could have been Baudelaire's: 'peut-être manqua-t-il le je ne sais quoi qui fait *un objet d'art d'un objet odieux*' (Delacroix's italics).[14]

Baudelaire wrote much on Delacroix's work, both in the *Salons* and in essays devoted to the painter. His treatment of one particular painting, Delacroix's *La Madeleine dans le désert*, is of particular relevance to our discussion. Consider the following short evocation from the *Salon de 1845*:

C'est une tête de femme renversée dans un cadre très étroit. À droite dans le haut, un petit bout de ciel ou de rocher — quelque chose de bleu; — les yeux de la Madeleine sont fermés, la bouche est molle et languissante, les cheveux épars. Nul, à moins de la voir, ne peut imaginer ce que l'artiste a mis de poésie intime, mystérieuse et romantique dans cette simple tête. (*OC* ii. 354)

In analysing 'Une martyre', we noted that a dynamic of voyeuristic objectification was created by setting the poetic objects inside a framed picture at which an onlooker was gazing. The prose description of the Delacroix painting (above) sets up these same structures for looking at the same type of object—a woman's head—but here the voyeur is straightforwardly the admiring Baudelaire.

The first sentence focuses on Mary Magdalene's head, decapitated, de-contextualized and fetishized by Baudelaire's tight framing of it in words, echoing the pictorial tight framing which he describes. As in the parallel drawn between the martyr's deadness (her blank gaze with its 'yeux révulsés') and her sexual appeal (the mention of her nakedness and her 'jarretière'), Baudelaire focuses here on the eyes which are 'fermés', suggesting death, and then on the wet volup-tuousness of the mouth. The same imaginative blending of eroticized blasphemy and rapturous ecstasy that we have seen in 'À une Madone' is visible in Delacroix's work, but more especially in Baudelaire's treatment of it.

Baudelaire's criticism of this painting is as much a piece of imaginative writing as is 'Une martyre'. *La Madeleine dans le désert* is a famously difficult painting to which to ascribe a meaning and intention, and contemporary critics were in disagreement as to Delacroix's aim and as to the 'aliveness' or deadness of the reclining woman.[15] Baudelaire takes from Delacroix's canvas certain elements of the image, which he carefully reconstitutes in his own map of desire. In the description of this painting, Baudelaire is interpreting a work of art from the perspective of perverse desire—his own. This suggests that the critical task is never a wholly impersonal or cold one, and that those elements of form and content that appear most effective and affective may mirror fundamental structures of desire shot through with the content of subjective fantasy. Indeed, Jules Buisson, a friend of Delacroix and Baudelaire, claimed that the artist complained of the gleeful attention paid by the poet to the morbid and destructive elements of his work.[16]

James Hiddleston, who discusses Baudelaire's writing on Delacroix's *Madeleine* in his recent book, agrees that 'Baudelaire recognized him-self in Delacroix, just as he was later to recognize himself in Poe'.[17] He declares, however, that 'Baudelaire's interpretation [...] should not be seen as an intrusion or an imposition of the poet's temperament upon an innocent work'.[18]

While I do not think that the work may be described as 'innocent' (indeed, I am not sure what this would mean), for me there is no doubt that Baudelaire appropriates Delacroix's morbid image, using it for his own imaginative forays into desire. Baudelaire's rhetoric betrays the intimate link he wants to forge between his own artistic project and Delacroix's. Whereas in 'Une martyre' Baudelaire will describe an imagined painting in words, here, in the description of La Madeleine (literally a painting), Baudelaire suggests that Delacroix's work contains elements of 'poésie intime, mystérieuse et romantique'. Elsewhere, he states of Delacroix that 'ses œuvres sont des poèmes, et de grands poèmes naïvement conçus' (*Salon de 1846*, *OC* ii. 431). On the one hand, we could read this rhetorical device as an echo of Gautier's desire for a rapprochement of pictorial and written art. On the other hand, a personal, wishful identification with Delacroix's fantasy world is very much in evidence here, suggesting that, for Baudelaire, the two artists transcend art forms in their shared aesthetic and libidinal vision.

In what may be his most famous essay on Baudelaire, Walter Benjamin focuses on the relation of the observer to the observed. He tells us that 'looking at someone carries the implicit expectation that our look will be returned'.[19] Baudelaire surrounds himself with poetic objects which, like the severed head of the martyr, do not look back at all. Their Medusan power is defused. The total projection onto the poetic object (and onto other artists) results in the thwarting of desire, which means that 'the expectation raised by the look of the human eye is not fulfilled'.[20]

Benjamin goes on: 'The deeper the remoteness which a glance has to overcome, the stronger will be the spell that is apt to emanate from the gaze. In eyes that look at us with a mirrorlike blankness the remoteness remains complete.'[21] To paraphrase Nietzsche, then, if you gaze for long enough into an abyss, the abyss will gaze also into you. This is both what the artist has wanted and what frustrates him. What looks back at us from a Baudelairean poem and from a Baudelairean essay on art are the deadness with which he has infused the textual object, and equally, the desire itself, traceable in the speaking gaps of the texts. Like Medusa's head, the self-conscious blinding venom of desire turns to stone what his pen touches. As in 'À celle qui est trop gaie', poisonous Baudelairean *jouissance* kills and stills both agent and victim. They fuse, and are dead together. There is no 'other' left, only reflections of 'my' desire.

Baudelaire's writing on this painter suggests a narcissistic concentration upon the images of his own desire, which are filtered through the visual substance of Delacroix's art, and given free imaginative rein, even in the dry task of the critical essay. The dying or dead *Madeleine* is transformed into an eroticized Baudelairean corpse, and the aesthetic judgement of the work is subordinated somewhat to a different level of appreciation. A close and demystifying consideration of Baudelaire's critical acclaim of Delacroix is fruitful for a reappraisal of the famous Baudelairean notion of transformation.

Some Concluding Remarks

Baudelaire's art criticism, as well as certain of the *Fleurs du Mal*, can be read as a complex series of attempts to embody the excess of desire in language. Baudelaire repetitively recasts encounters with death through a progression of scenarios in which otherness is annihilated, while the ego—frustratingly—remains. What Bersani posits as just one element of Baudelaire's desiring persona can in fact be seen to describe a central organizing tenet of his artistic and psychical project. Baudelaire addresses the moment at which self-destructive urges become intersubjective, libidinized attempts at union. The corpses imagined, created and dissected in these poems are at once monuments and ciphers, transformations of the other, and pheno-menological mirroring devices through which the poetic persona glimpses, vicariously, a vision of self-destruction. As we have seen in 'Une martyre', the corpse marks the end point of the imaginative journey, it celebrates stasis and an impasse in comprehension. Yet, despite this, it continues to resonate with a significance that the watcher in the poem—and the reader—cannot fully possess.

My intention in this chapter has not been to reduce Baudelaire's œuvre to the repetitive reiteration of pathological sexual obsession. Rather, I hope to have deepened and enlarged critical appreciation of Baudelaire by showing a previously understudied continuum in his production. My reading has attempted to account psychoanalytically and phenomenologically for certain aspects of the traditionally under-stood character of 'the Baudelairean', and to add a new perspective to the wealth of existing theorization and criticism of this widely acclaimed writer. According to Freud, the creative mental work of idealizing transformation is the prerequisite of both extreme per-version and art. These poems enact the sexual equivalent of looking into the abyss. They describe a compulsive drive for transformation and counter-transformation ad infinitum. In Baudelaire's poetry, the many shocks and traumas encountered by the reader can be seen as the results of the writer's thwarted ambition to leap recklessly, through the other, into death.

Notes to Chapter 3

1. Georges Blin dedicates a full-length volume to Baudelaire's debt to Sade and treatment of sadistic themes, in *Le Sadisme de Baudelaire* (Paris: Corti, 1948). In *Poésie et profondeur* (Paris: Seuil, 1955), Jean-Pierre Richard discusses Baudelaire's sadism as a controlling mechanism in a paradoxical attempt to eliminate excess and inequality.

2. Marie Bonaparte, 'Deuil, nécrophilie et sadisme à propos d'Edgar Poe', *Revue française de psychanalyse* 4 (1930–1), 716–34 (732).

3. See my discussion of his ideas above in Chapter 2 (p. 50).

4. Leo Bersani, *Baudelaire and Freud* (Berkeley: University of California Press, 1977), 89.

5. Jean-Paul Sartre, *Baudelaire* (Paris: Gallimard, 1946), 126.

6. See R. Greaves, *Nadar ou le paradoxe vital* (Paris: Flammarion, 1980).

7. Janine Chasseguet-Smirgel, *Creativity and Perversion* (London: Free Association Books, 1985), 12.

8. Roman Jakobson and Morris Halle, *Fundamentals of Language* (The Hague: Mouton, 1956), 76–82.

9. An example is Hugo's seminal poem 'Réponse à un acte d'accusation', in which he advocates the use of any word in the service of poetic endeavour. Rimbaud's 'Les Chercheuses de poux' and 'Le Bateau ivre' are also notable for the poeticization of unlikely words or subject matter.

10. Bersani, *Baudelaire and Freud*, 73.

11. Blin, *Le Sadisme de Baudelaire*, 31 (my italics).

12. 'À celle qui est trop gaie' was the first of the tribute poems which Baudelaire sent anonymously to Mme Sabatier in 1852. On discovering the identity of her suitor, following the publication of *Les Fleurs du Mal*, Sabatier returned his affection wholeheartedly. This seems rather extraordinary. We can either assume that she understood the murderous implication of the poem's closing lines to be no more than a literary joke, or that she was in some way flattered by or receptive to the described formulation of desire. Either way, this re-emphasizes my point that these poems are love poems, in this case used actively in the service of the poet's extra-diegetic libidinal aims.

13. 'Porphyria's Lover', in *Robert Browning: The Poems*, ed. John Pettigrew and T. J. Collins, 2 vols. (Harmondsworth: Penguin, 1981), i. 380–1.

14. Eugène Delacroix, *Journal 1822–1863* [1931–2], ed. André Joubin (Paris: Plon, 1980), 5 Mar. 1849, p. 182.

15. A. Houssaye wonders in 1845 'si c'est la figure d'une femme qui rêve, d'une femme qui dort, ou d'une femme qui vient de mourir'. P. Haussard considers it 'une admirable étude d'une jeune femme morte, que le sentiment et la châleur n'ont pas tout-à-fait abandonnée', while J. Joseph describes Mary Magdalene's state as 'une agonie tranquillisée'. All cited in *The Paintings of Eugène Delacroix: A Critical Catalogue: 1832–63* (text), ed. Lee Johnson, 3 vols. (Oxford: Clarendon Press, 1986), iii. 217–18.

16. See Lois Boe Hyslop, *Baudelaire, Man of his Time* (New Haven: Yale University Press, 1980), 14.

17. James Hiddleston, *Baudelaire and the Art of Memory* (Oxford: Oxford University Press, 1999), 55.

18. Ibid., 54.
19. Walter Benjamin, 'On some motifs in Baudelaire', in *Illuminations: Essays and Reflections*, trans. Harry Zohn (London: Jonathan Cape, 1970), 190.
20. Ibid., 191.
21. Ibid., 192.

CHAPTER 4

Rachilde and the Death of Gender

> Le dégoût de la femme! La haine de la force mâle! Voici que
> certains cerveaux rêvent d'un être insexué. Ces imaginations
> sentent la mort.
>
> MAURICE BARRÈS[1]

Rachilde belongs to that category of writers who, celebrated in their
own lifetime, fall into obscurity for a period of some decades
following their death, until the preoccupations of their Zeitgeist again
become fashionable or seem pertinent for dissection by a new generation of readers and critics. Heralded by her Decadent contemporaries, Rachilde is now being reassessed by scholars as an important
female writer and an early exponent of theories regarding the
flexibility of categories of gender and sexuality.

Rachilde gained notoriety among her peers owing to the *succès de
scandale* surrounding the publication and prosecution of *Monsieur
Vénus* in Belgium in 1884. Maurice Barrès nicknamed her 'Mademoiselle Baudelaire', an allusion to her exploitation of such typically
Baudelairean themes as sexual deviance, death and murder.
Throughout her literary production, Rachilde plays with techniques
of inverting gender expectations and stereotypes, most obviously seen
in the titles of her novels *Monsieur Vénus*, *La Marquise de Sade* (1887)
and *Madame Adonis* (1888). Many of the novels feature strong female
protagonists who display independent and unconventional sexual
behaviour. (Who could forget the description of the heroine of *La
Jongleuse* (1900) achieving sexual climax with her huge vase, while her
would-be suitor looks jealously on?)

Barrès's preface to the 1929 Flammarion edition of *Monsieur Vénus*
dwells on the 'extraordinary' fact of a 20-year-old girl producing a
work of such perversity: 'La maladie du siècle, qu'il faut toujours citer

et dont *Monsieur Vénus* signale chez la femme une des formes les plus intéressantes, est faite en effet d'une fatigue nerveuse, excessive et d'un orgueil inconnu jusqu'alors.'[2] The unease revealed here by the pathologizing language provides a good indication of the typical attitude of the age regarding 'appropriate' feminine behaviour and the question of female creativity. It says as much about male expectations as it does about Rachilde's writing.

Rachilde's combination of textual audacity and female authorship has proved controversial for a readership extending beyond her male contemporaries. The efflorescence of twentieth-century feminist research on Rachilde has revealed a somewhat ambivalent reception. For Jennifer Birkett[3] and, more recently, Diana Holmes[4] and Alison Finch,[5] Rachilde's writing is guilty of repeating male Decadent assumptions about the monstrous woman and the destructive 'natural' power of the feminine. For Birkett, Rachilde's feisty female protagonists are not empowered figures but reflections of 'male masochistic fantasies'. Their actions are not authentic but signal instead 'the temporary triumph of the vengeful female and the humiliating overthrow of the male'.[6]

For me, such a statement is problematic on two counts. Firstly, it risks an essentialist claim along the lines that sadism and a desire for power can never be authentic for the feminine subject. To delineate conflict, tension and power as belonging only to the masculine imaginary risks a narrow and limiting definition of the feminine as soft-focus, bland and undifferentiated. Secondly, I am uncomfortable with critical responses which place an (impossible) burden upon writers from marginalized groups (female, gay, black) to produce only positive, healthy, life-affirming representations of these groups. As the best-known and certainly most prolific female writer of her day, Rachilde risks having an unrealistic responsibility to represent 'Everywoman' fall to her posthumously.

The role of modern feminist spokeswoman was, in fact, one that Rachilde wilfully rejected. Criticisms are often levelled at her for her apolitical stance and her refusal to engage with the question of female emancipation, as seen in her 1928 text *Pourquoi je ne suis pas féministe*. Dressing as a man and signing herself 'Rachilde, homme de lettres', the writer enjoyed for herself privileges that were ordinarily forbidden to her sex. Rather than working for large-scale change for the social category of women, she sought instead to exempt herself from that category, to become an honorary man.

Diana Holmes comments on the futility of Rachilde's attempts to function and write outside her gender position:

As a writer, she insisted on her transcendence of her sex [...] but she wrote, inevitably, out of a vision of the world emotionally, psychologically, intellectually shaped by the experience of a female subject in a highly gendered culture. Rachilde's deliberate, impassioned disturbance of the rules of gender is just one of the ways in which, paradoxically, she writes 'as a woman'.[7]

Rachilde's arch individualism and rejection of cultural constraints must also be understood in the light of her affiliation with Decadent aesthetic philosophy. The glorification of the individual (Barrès's *culte du moi*) is a symptom of the rejection of communality and the social imperative in Decadence. The implications of this apolitical stance are certainly not unproblematic—it was precisely the pose of the wealthy, aristocratic male. Rachilde's attempt to appropriate this position in her writing can be interpreted either as radical *mauvaise foi* or as a celebration of the freedom afforded by the space of creative endeavour. While her politics in the world were elitist and conservative, it is possible to read Rachilde's art as a space for imaginative experimentation with the limits and possibilities of identity and desire.

Women in Rachilde's texts are certainly allowed to say and do things that women in Rachilde's society were not. In *La Marquise de Sade*, Mary Barbe announces to her new husband her unwillingness to provide him with a son and heir: 'Louis, je suis décidée à ne pas vous donner d'héritier [...] Je ne veux ni enlaidir ni souffrir. De plus, *je suis assez*, EN ÉTANT, et si je pouvais finir le monde avec moi, je le finirais.'[8] Sexuality for Mary is wholly in the service of (sadistic) pleasure rather than reproduction. The repetitive iteration of 'moi' in the voices of her female characters becomes recognizable as the voice of selfish desire articulating its being. In this, Rachilde resists equally the imperative to conform to society's expectations of the passive maternal wife and feminism's call to sisterhood and collective arms. Rachilde's singular voice is, at different moments, triumphant, lonely and brave. It is certainly characterized by the sterile destructivity of the solipsist. But, as I shall go on to explore, it is destructive always in the pursuit of a vision of pleasure.

I am not the first to suggest that the main interest of Rachilde's texts lie in her ability to create literary models of perverse desire, rather than in her value as a social commentator or political spokeswoman. As her biographer Claude Dauphiné comments: 'Peu de critiques comprirent que *Monsieur Vénus* et plus encore *La Marquise de Sade* [...] étaient l'illustration littéraire de manuels de psycho-pathologie sexuelle.'[9] Rachilde's portrayal of sexual perversion can at times be read as a mocking and knowing wink in the direction of the writers of sexological texts. At other times, however, she creates profoundly affective literary embodiments of the movements and interruptions of desire. In exploring the vagaries of perverse desire, Rachilde is as sincere, tireless and as comprehensive as Sade.

This chapter will focus in detail on three of Rachilde's novels, beginning with her best-known work, *Monsieur Vénus*. The novel will be explored with regard to its games of gender inversion and power play. I shall challenge readings which claim that these textual games constitute the 'point' of this work, and shall instead foreground the importance of the novel's ending, which constitutes death rather than gender as the privileged system by which desire works. The second text for consideration will be *La Tour d'amour* (1899). This is often considered Rachilde's most proficient and effective novel.[10] It is also one of the few existing full-length novelistic explorations of necrophilia in Western literature. The chapter will close with a reading of *Le Grand Saigneur* (1922) which will entail a discussion of the relation between the mythic figure of the vampire and necrophilia.

Le Grand Saigneur will be the last and the most recent literary work discussed at length in the present study, and it will have been noted that its date extends beyond the end of the nineteenth century. My inclusion of it here is both in the interests of thematic unity and comprehensiveness, as it is wholly relevant to the subject under discussion, and to suggest some continuum between the centuries. A brief discussion of the legacy of nineteenth-century necrophilia in the twentieth century will follow in the conclusion.

Monsieur Vénus: the Mutability of Identity

Monsieur Vénus tells the story of the relationship between Raoule de Vénérande, an independent young aristocrat, and Jacques Silvert, an effete, struggling artist who often works for his sister Marie as a maker of artificial flowers. The attribution of unlikely professions and social positions to male and female characters is just one of the ways in which Rachilde systematically destabilizes and inverts stereotypes of gender in *Monsieur Vénus* and other works.

The theme of gender inversion in *Monsieur Vénus* is sustained by means of a rather complicated play with linguistic signifiers. Raoule's guardian—her aunt—refers to Raoule as 'son neveu'.[11] The conceit develops as Raoule arrives at Jacques's studio wearing a 'costume presque masculin' (*MV* 56) and demands access to his body in the guise of bathing him. Her justification for gazing upon his body is expressed thus: 'Mais souvenez-vous donc que je suis un garçon, moi, disait-elle, un artiste que ma tante appelle son neveu' (*MV* 57). Jacques's naming of Raoule 'Monsieur de Vénérande' (*MV* 59) performs the final step in undoing the couple's gender.[12]

This game with language continues, as in the scene where Raoule confesses her love for Jacques to de Raittolbe, her would-be suitor:

> — Ami, dit-elle brusquement, *je suis amoureux*!
> [...]
> — Sapho! ... Allons, ajouta-t-il avec un geste ironique, je m'en doutais. Continuez, monsieur de Vénérande, continuez, *mon* cher ami!
> [...]
> — Vous vous trompez, monsieur de Raittolbe; être Sapho, ce serait être tout le monde! (*MV* 90)

This is a very rich piece of dialogue. Raoule's place in masculine society is confirmed here as she confesses her unconventional love affair to Raittolbe, professing herself 'amoureux' rather than 'amoureuse'. When Raittolbe responds by calling her 'monsieur', he promotes her to a position of homosocial bonding. That is, she and Raittolbe discuss sexuality and 'the prey' on equal ground, the difference between them removed.

Although gendered names and titles are seen to be meaningful here, in so far as they are the way in which society constitutes identity and power, we may note that, in the passage quoted above, Raoule rejects the label of 'lesbian'. I would argue that this is not simply because Raoule finds the term inaccurate (i.e. she doesn't identify as a woman loving another woman). Rather, emphasis is being placed on the inadequacy of such categories as 'lesbian' to convey the individuality of desire. While 'lesbian' is an understood identity, Raoule claims to have discovered 'un amour tout neuf' (*MV* 93). She proclaims herself as a sexual innovator, a pioneer in territories of perversion as yet uncharted.[13]

This renunciation of categories prefigures by a hundred years Judith Butler's deconstruction of gender and sexual identity, succinctly summed up in the following formula: 'There are no direct expressive or causal links between sex, gender, gender presentation, sexual practice, fantasy and sexuality. None of these terms captures or determines the rest.'[14] Where Butler is suspicious of these fixed terms for reasons that are largely political, Rachilde is more concerned with the metaphysical and ontological inaccuracies they imply.

Consider the words spoken by Raoule a few pages later: 'on ne m'a pas donné assez de jouissances pour que mon cerveau n'ait pas eu le loisir de chercher mieux ... J'ai voulu *l'impossible* ... Je le possède ... C'est-à-dire non, je ne le posséderai jamais!' (*MV* 95) and 'j'aimerais Jacques comme un fiancé aime sans espoir la fiancée morte!' (97). Beyond the obvious meaning of these words—that sexual intercourse will not play a part in their relationship—we may read another level of talking about desire. It is unusual to see 'jouissances' in the plural, where it means 'orgasm' rather than simply 'enjoyment'. This has the effect of diminishing the power and pleasure of genital orgasm, rendering it banal, ten-a-penny—in short, attainable. These multiple and unimpressive orgasms are juxtaposed to the image of the dead fiancée, so that once again the image of a dead love object appears as a figure for the impossibility of fulfilling desire. The 'impossible' would be a pleasure that is infinitely lasting yet simultaneously capable of being sated.

This formulation puts into the shade the game with gender pronouns, which would imply a belief that masculinity and femininity are stable terms and that they retain an essential association with activity and passivity, even if one transposes the objects to which they are applied. The multiple mentions of the annihilation of gender, the rejection of both heterosexuality and homosexuality, and the image of a dead fiancée as ideal object suggest a specific configuration of death-driven desire.

I would contend that this novel is trying to think outside gender, yet it does this—paradoxically—by playing very deliberately with the binary signifiers of gender, breaking them down and showing that they are inadequate as a system of meaning. The strongest proof of this in the text comes in the figure of Raoule's marriage to Jacques—the gendered institution par excellence. The game of inversion continues to be exploited in the description of the wedding party: 'Vers minuit, les invités [...] s'aperçurent d'un fait bien étrange: la jeune mariée était encore parmi eux, mais le jeune marié avait disparu' (*MV* 201). The tradition of marriage is parodied by such elements as the amusing details of Jacques's 'becoming' coyness. Also, the symbols of the married state are deliberately exaggerated, such as the sumptuous marital chamber that Raoule has constructed for the couple with its statue of Eros—a marital chamber in which the prescribed rite of married couples will never take place.

It is during the wedding night that the schism will occur in the union of Jacques and Raoule, where previously they have been 'la seule divinité de l'amour en deux personnes' (*MV* 187). The nuptial bed brings demystification for Jacques, when during an embrace, Raoule's breasts are inadvertently uncovered:

— Raoule, s'écria Jacques, la face convulsée [...] tu n'es donc pas un homme? tu ne peux donc pas être un homme?

Et le sanglot des illusions détruites, pour toujours mortes, monta de ses flancs à sa gorge. (*MV* 216)

Not only Raoule's bosom is revealed here, but also the mismatch between Raoule's and Jacques's perception. For Raoule, desire is essentially cerebral and the reality of bodies irrelevant, beyond their surface appearance as art objects.

Jacques's failure to suspend disbelief in this crucial moment will lead to a waning of his loyalty to Raoule and a progressive promiscuity, culminating in his attempted seduction of Raittolbe, when s/he goes to visit him 'en costume de femme' (*MV* 234). The suggestion is that Jacques's feminization has left him with not only the 'heart of a woman', but the characteristics of Freud's classic figure of the polymorphously perverse woman corrupted by a perverted lover.[15] Biological sex clearly retains the association of power for Jacques, suggesting that his own male sex is the one symbol of the order of reality that he is able to deny (a Lacanian would be amused by this rare case of having the phallus and not wanting it).

Ultimately, then, Jacques is unable to recognize Raoule's desire. He sought to escape through their relationship from his masculine gender role, while she sought to escape from the system of gender altogether. To satisfy her, he would have to be not just her 'femme' but the 'fiancée morte'. For Raoule, Jacques had become 'sa chose, une sorte d'être inerte' (*MV* 115). This description prefigures the only possible erotic resort that would meet her criteria of desire: a necrophilic resolution.

The supposed honour and chivalry of the masculine rite of the duel is amusingly debunked by Rachilde. Following Jacques's unsuccessful attempt to seduce Raittolbe, honour demands that the two 'men' should settle their differences in armed combat. However, Raoule intervenes and perverts the code by whispering her order to Raittolbe: '— A mort! jeta-t-elle simplement dans l'oreille de Raittolbe' (*MV* 236). While Jacques's death comes about in a socially approved way—by means of a duel—the real agent of destruction is Raoule, who awaits the completion of the 'dirty work' in order to act out the next stage of her libidinal plan.

Consider the following passage from the final pages of *Monsieur Vénus* describing the *chambre close* of the Hôtel de Vénérande:

Cette chambre est toute bleue comme un ciel sans nuages. Sur la couche en forme de conque, gardée par un Eros de marbre, repose un mannequin de cire revêtu d'un épiderme de caoutchouc transparent. Les cheveux roux, les cils blonds, le duvet d'or de la poitrine sont naturels; les dents qui ornent la bouche, les ongles des mains et des pieds ont été arrachés à un cadavre. Les yeux en émail ont un adorable regard.

[...]

La nuit, une femme vêtue de deuil, quelquefois un jeune homme en habit noir, ouvrent cette porte.

Ils viennent s'agenouiller près du lit, et, lorsqu'ils ont longtemps contemplé les formes merveilleuses de la statue de cire, ils l'enlacent, la baisent aux lèvres. Un ressort, disposé à l'intérieur des flancs, correspond à la bouche et l'anime.

Ce mannequin, chef-d'œuvre d'anatomie, a été fabriqué par un Allemand. (*MV* 246–7)

The figure of the corpse-doll—half human flesh, half machine, beautiful automaton—is a typical image of the Decadent aesthetic, as described in Villiers de l'Isle-Adam's *L'Ève future* (1886). But also, it must be noted that it comes of a long tradition of such figures, back to the early years of the century with Hoffmann's *Der Sandmann* (1809). Like the figure of the androgyne, celebrated in much nineteenth-century French fiction, from Balzac's 'Sarrasine' to Rachilde's various desirable wo/men, the automaton is a figure of titillation. Promising more than it can offer, seeming to be what it is not, ripe with association and empty of definite meaning or identity, it seems to epitomize the nature of the ideal sexual object. Between death and life, reality and unreality, it is a liminal site on which desire may be exercised. The doll in Jacques's image is a figure of perfect passivity with the perverse elements of a bespoke sex toy, an object of pure pleasure and indulgence for the possessor.

With her half-organic, half-mechanical corpse, Raoule has found the ultimate symbol of the ambiguity that her desirous economy seeks. The figure of the necrophilic lover is sometimes a woman in mourning and sometimes a young man: 'she' ('elle', sometimes 'il') has become 'they' ('ils'). This pluralization of Raoule's persona suggests a novelistic version of the process of incorporation. Raoule's lover, whom she has always wanted to belong to her entirely, now inhabits her internal as well as external space, and their union continues in the schizoid desirous economy of the imagination.

The abolition of difference that Raoule attempted by deconstructing gender positions has its inevitable outcome in this annihilation of all resistance. The difference that is gender can, to some extent, be overcome, but the aim of this desire seems to be to overcome difference per se, so that the living presence of an other must be sacrificed for the vicarious pleasure of the one. In the creation of her character Raoule, with whose subjectivity the narrative is closely aligned, Rachilde has attempted to demonstrate the outcome of an attempt to obliterate more than gender difference. In fact, the novel can be read as a structural map of deathly desire, in which the possibility of reproductive sexual relations is wholly replaced by a sterile and cerebrally driven passion for possession and annihilation.

Necrophilia as Narrative: *La Tour d'amour*

La Tour d'amour is the tale of a young man, Jean le Malreux, disappointed in love (as his surname would suggest), who takes a new job as second lighthouse-keeper on the Tour Ar-men. The novel charts his relationship with the head lighthouse-keeper, Mathurin Barnabas, who is first presented as an eccentric and bizarre figure, and slowly revealed as a practising necrophile who enjoys the bodies of female shipwreck victims. The setting at sea and the descriptions of the work of the lighthouse keepers form a constant backdrop against which, and in tune with which, the emotional vacillations of the men are evoked. The claustrophobic atmosphere is only slightly broken by the three excursions to the mainland made by Malreux when he goes in search of a wife.

In his chapter on Rachilde's technique as a novelist, Dauphiné claims tantalizingly that *La Tour d'amour* is a 'véritable exercice de style sur la nécrophilie'.[16] Unfortunately, he does not go on to explain what he means by this or to undertake a reading of Rachilde's novel in this light. Such a reading, then, will be the task which falls to me in this section of the present chapter.

There is very little action or plot development in the novel, other than personal and intersubjective revelations. Rather, it reads like a surreal dream structured around chains of association and the powerful evocation of atmosphere. It is lyrical and punctuated by transports of rapturous prose which mirror the subject matter of dream, fantasy and illusion. The fact that the novel is written in the first person and that the revelations of the novel are presented from Malreux's perspective means that Rachilde's voice is less forceful in this text than in *Monsieur Vénus*. Many of her observations are filtered through Malreux's consciousness and there is no direct authorial intervention.

The primary textual association—that of Mathurin Barnabas with death and femininity—is established from the outset by the plethora of images and similes linking him to a corpse, and most strikingly to a female corpse. From their first meeting, Malreux is struck by his appearance and comments on 'sa face de vieille morte'[17] and 'sa sacrée tête de moribonde' (*TA* 40). Moreover, in the evenings, Barnabas wears a bizarre helmet on which are fixed two long, blond plaits of hair, and the sound of his singing is mistaken by Malreux for the voice of a woman (40).

On the level of subjective experience, the text intercuts images of Barnabas seen and described from Malreux's viewpoint with Malreux's internal fantasy and dream world, which is often intensely eroticized. Having observed Barnabas dressing up in his 'casquette', Malreux dreams of a woman: 'Je rêvai des choses curieuses. D'abord, je vis revenir de l'esplanade une belle fille qui fredonnait. Elle tenait un couteau, celui du vieux, et elle me le posa tout doucement le long de la nuque' (*TA* 54). An object belonging to Barnabas suggests a deadly erotic encounter, which is then lived in dream with Malreux playing the role of the victim.

This internal state of delirium is soon projected outwards, so that the environment of the monolithic lighthouse surrounded by the sea becomes a signifier for sexual isolation, melding the internal and external into one overpowering image of vertiginous absence: 'En bas, la mer se roulait, chantant son chant de mort, étendant, de places noires en places noires, ses linges blancs, tout préparés pour la dernière toilette des hommes d'équipages. Ce singulier vertige, que j'avais déjà éprouvé étant assis sur l'esplanade, me tournait encore la tête. Oui, je me sentais toujours attiré dans le vide ...' (*TA* 66). The description of the dream foregrounds a sense of sexual loss. (Malreux's only previous lover, a Maltese girl, has been unfaithful and he broods constantly upon her memory.) The idea of loss becomes interchangeable with the symbol of the sea in which sailors lose themselves. Losing oneself (to death or rapture) is a constant motif in *La Tour d'amour*.

A major structural feature of the text is the interchangeability or identification between characters, symbols and objects, which relies on a system of associations being established. From contemplation of the sea as the deathbed of seafarers, Malreux goes on to liken the world of his dream to the sea, and thereby to identify himself with the drowned sailors, in a collapsing of ego boundaries which characterizes the novel: 'J'avais la sensation d'être encore dans mon rêve, de dormir et de rouler selon le bercement des vagues ténébreuses, un bord sur l'autre, me moquant bien de la réalité' (*TA* 67). The chain of collapsing connections comes full circle with the sound of Barnabas's singing, which cuts into these dream-like musings:

> 'C'est la tour prends garde!
> 'C'est la tour d'amour ... ou ... our ... ur!'
> La voix montait, se mêlait au vent et devenait lointaine comme celle d'une fille qu'on étranglerait sur les dunes pendant une nuit d'équinoxe. (*TA* 98)

Here, firstly, Barnabas's voice is collapsed onto the surrounding environment—it is part of the sound of the wind. Then, it is not only like a woman's voice, but explicitly like that of a woman being killed in this evocative image of sexual murder.

By this point, the necrophilic nature of the pattern of imagery that is forming becomes overt. The figurative vocabulary of dead or fatal women, the description of Barnabas's face and voice, his behaviour and the language woven around him all point to an identification between a necrophile and his victim. Also explicit is the incorporation of Malreux into the strange erotic life of the 'tour d'amour' and the surrounding elements, seen in his dreams and the breaking down of his subjective identity in such descriptions as this one of a sea storm:

> On n'a pas d'idée de ce que c'est que la pluie en mer, et sur un phare. Ça brouille tout, ça mouille tout, ça vous fond la cervelle, ça vous dilue les moelles, on coule, on s'égoutte peu à peu, on est moins consistant qu'un nuage, n'importe quel prétexte vous serait bon pour aller rejoindre l'eau, la grande eau finale. (*TA* 105)

The images of dissolution here are linked and made equivalent by a series of commas, enacting the idea of boundaries breaking down and of identities losing their individuality. The 'tour d'amour' is not just the physical setting of the novel, but the symbol of a very particular kind of erotic consciousness, characterized by colossal phallic power (the all-male atmosphere of a lighthouse watch) which is slowly eroded and beaten down by the abyssal surrounding sea. By analogy, 'healthy' heterosexual desire is slowly collapsed into a death-driven longing for eternal union with the beyond. Rachilde's depiction of the Tour Ar-men is the closest thing I have found to a representation of necrophile community.

The first real event of the novel, which disrupts the repetitive refrains of association, mood and emotion described above, is a shipwreck. Having watched the row of male corpses float to the surface of the water and past the lighthouse, Malreux begins to wonder why there are no female victims. Even before he has a material answer to this puzzle, his unconscious mind provides him with one: 'Je rêvais qu'une morte noyée ... qui avait les cheveux du vieux, ses cheveux du soir ...' (*TA* 119). The punctuation here reveals hesitation on Malreux's part. The *points de suspension* and the unfinished sentence mark a textual encounter with the unsayable. While this may be Rachilde's attempt to convey simple coyness on Malreux's part, it is equally likely that the unspoken content of the thought is a desire which remains repressed, which fears to surface. Having fed us the textual clues of the content of Malreux's dream life in many previous passages, Rachilde has awoken certain expectations in the reader. That which is not articulated speaks out loudly.

In fact, the dream is prophetic, and the next day, while looking for Barnabas, Malreux discovers an object which 'paraissait si blanc, si pur, si allongé en forme de fuseau et si joli' (*TA* 125). It is a naked female corpse, 'jambes d'un côté, bras de l'autre' (124). The textual supplanting of Barnabas by the corpse—Malreux looks for one and finds the other—suggests again the equivalence at the textual level that Rachilde wants to imply between 'doer' and 'done-to', and reminds us of the proximity that the necrophile feels to the victim.

The coming to the surface of the female corpse signals a coming to the surface of Malreux's consciousness of Barnabas's desirous identity. The white female flesh is described in terms of a disordered series of part-objects, which gain cohesion only when Malreux realizes their significance: 'c'est une femme! criai-je' (*TA* 125). Similarly, when he confronts Barnabas with his discovery, he finally dares to believe his suspicions. By voicing them, bringing them to the surface of discourse, he makes them real: 'nous nous étions enfin compris' (128).

The second major event of the novel is Malreux's shore leave, which follows directly on his understanding of Barnabas's position. He resolves to find himself a wife and to leave the 'tour d'amour' behind forever. The town symbolizes an alternative conscious state to that of the tower. Malreux is charmed by the childish innocence of the innkeeper's daughter and resolves to make her his wife. This section attempts to highlight the life-driven eroticism of Malreux, but it is hard for the reader to forget his dreams and the image of the girl being strangled. Similarly, when the Bretonne kisses Malreux, the imagery chosen by Rachilde reveals emotional ambivalence: 'C'était le baiser breton, le roi de tous les baisers, celui qui enivre les fiancés chastes ... ou qui les tue!' (*TA* 154). The constant mention of death associated with love suggests a close liaison or proximity between the type of desire represented by Barnabas and the healthy manifestation of living sexuality to which Malreux clings.

Indeed, on return to the tower, the identification between Barnabas and Malreux will increase, despite the latter's attempts to distance himself from Barnabas by way of his project of marriage and procreative sexuality. In fact, when Malreux dreams of his fiancée on the first night back in the tower, the link is assured: 'L'Amour? Peu à peu cette maigre petite fille grandissait au-dessus de la mer. Elle se dressait devant le phare, elle venait à moi, soulevant le tulle blanc de l'écume pour s'en faire des fichus neufs. [...] Elle était belle, bien plus belle que les femmes des naufrages qui sont nues, les cheveux étalés en arrière de leur corps' (*TA* 160). The mention of the naked corpse (already prefigured by the emergence of the little Bretonne from a watery grave like a deathly image of Venus) instantly suggests the link between the two in Malreux's mind, even as he attempts to negate it in the last statement. In fact, the dream has a clearly revelatory quality, as Rachilde will have Malreux admit: 'le jeune fou qui aime est semblable au vieux fou qui se souvient' (*TA* 161).

The notion of remembering suggests that Barnabas's necrophilia has the character of a repetitive and renewable ritual. On Malreux's return, the blond plaits have gone and the casquette is now adorned with dark tufts (grotesquely figured as 'les deux oreilles de chien épagneul', *TA* 158) which he has clearly stripped from the most recent *naufragée*. The relic of hair is a sensuous symbol of remembrance, a talisman of erotic memory. Memory activated by symbols is an omnipresent feature of the text. We are told that Barnabas lost the ability to read on the night that Malreux's predecessor died (in mysterious circumstances), suggesting the fragility of memory in the face of shock or emotional instability. The constant repetition of images in the novel, as well as the resurgence of emotional revelations and of relics being washed up to the surface of the sea, foreground this notion of remembrance, trauma and ritual.

Just what is it that Barnabas remembers with each of his fresh corpses? We, remembering Freud, may suspect that this search for new objects repeats the quest for an original object. He hints at a founding memory, the origin of his present state, and mentions two important women in his life: the dead women he keeps locked up in a hidden cupboard in the tower, and the woman to whom he was once married: 'Je m'avais marié dans le temps jadis, maintenant, personne, mon gars, ne peut plus me tromper. Elles sont meilleures filles que les autres et elles parlent pas ... c'est tout miel' (TA 174). The mention of infidelity on the part of his first love creates another link with Malreux's own erotic history. Also, given their constant assimilation and association, the reader cannot but suspect that the two women mentioned by Barnabas may be one and the same.

This notion of the living and the dead object of affection being the same is again represented in Malreux's musings before bedtime. He remembers a dark birthmark on his Maltese girlfriend's throat and wonders where he has seen this combination of pallor and darkness recently. Suddenly, the revelation comes: 'La noyée! Tonnerre de sort!' (TA 180). The chain of connections persists in dream: 'En m'endormant, je guignais la photographie de la mauresque de Malte, je pensais à ma jolie petite promise, mais ... mais ce fut la noyée qui me suça les moelles du fond d'un cauchemar atroce, ce fut la noyée du vieux qui m'eut tout entier, corps et âme. Parce que les mystères des rêves sont les avertissements de Dieu' (TA 180).

Malreux is to visit his fiancée the next day, but it is of a dead woman that he dreams. We notice a progression in Malreux's dream women, from an erotic knife-wielding femme fatale, to a sea-dwelling Venus who was 'better than' Barnabas's corpses, to the triumph of the necrophilic imagination seen here, where the drowned woman has the ultimate appeal. This progression may be more properly read as a regression, as the surfacing of deeply hidden desires.

The notion of dream as a warning from God is one way of encoding the idea of dream as a revelation of the unconscious's true desires and impulses. In fact, the dream does prove to be a warning of doom, When Malreux arrives at the inn, the little girl is not waiting for him, and, in a morbid mood of introspection, he announces himself 'mort aux filles' (*TA* 187).

On his second return to the tower, Malreux has arrived at a position of understanding: 'Je n'aimais pas cette petite fille de Brest, plus que j'avais aimé les petites filles de Malte. J'aimais ... l'Amour' (*TA* 187). This formula suggests a conscious foregrounding of the 'essence of desire' on the part of Rachilde. It posits a notion of love which is always figured through projections, imagination and compensation for inner feelings of loss. It understands that desire has to do with a relation more to self than to other, and that the necessary other will always fall short of the self's expectations.

This formula figures desire as the eternal state of loss in which the subject must constantly search for a missing object. The search for the 'essential something' comes to centre on Malreux's fascination with the dead woman locked in the cupboard, of which Barnabas has spoken ('Voilà que la curiosité me tourmentait d'ouvrir', *TA* 193). This privileged corpse, which is preserved and hidden from sight, becomes a signifier for desire *tout court*. The unseen has the power of suspending disappointment and disillusionment and promising all riches. Malreux is aware that his curiosity is leading him dangerously close to a perhaps unbearable self-truth: 'J'aurais dû persévérer dans mes bonnes résolutions de mariage. C'était ça le salut ... mais quelque chose d'inexplicable s'emparait de moi. Un vertige, le *délire du vent*, ou l'appétit du chagrin' (*TA* 195). Hence, rather than pursuing the palliative of 'ordinary' sexual desire, enjoyment and subsequent disappointment, Malreux chooses to dwell close to this talismanic emblem of loss which begins to bring him the masochistic pleasure of denying himself ('Je me sentais si malheureux, si triste, que je souhaitais l'être davantage', *TA* 195).

Rachilde's evocation of dream once again suggests Malreux's fascination with the icon of the female corpse as symbol of nostalgic, remembered, impossible love:

Mes nuits sont affreuses, je vois des figures lamentables se coller contre la vitre de mon hublot. Des dames blanches, éplorées sous leurs cheveux noirs, me font signe de les suivre, elles me glacent de leurs yeux morts, pleins d'eau verte; dès que je me lève pour les aller chasser, elles reculent effrayées, à leur tour, de me voir, s'enfuient éperdues, leur longue chevelure battant leur dos, et je suis assez lâche pour les supplier de rester.

Ce n'est plus aux femmes vivantes que je songe. Il me faudrait des créatures plus passives, plus complaisantes, plus au-dessus des pudeurs de ce monde pour m'amuser maintenant, ou, alors, de telles filles dévergondées, possédant de tels secrets d'amour! (*TA* 203–4)

In this long passage of dream-description, the symbols of life-driven eroticism that we saw earlier on have been subsumed into the out-pouring of the death-driven imagination. The notions of insatiable desire and the unattainable object are maintained in the elusiveness of the dream corpses which 's'enfuient' to avoid Malreux's embrace. The rejection of living girls in favour of the 'secrets d'amour' possessed by the dead is a figure for the abandonment of one model of desire in favour of another. By manipulating the descriptions of his dream women, Rachilde has her protagonist grappling with the slipperiness of fantasy.

I have shown that throughout the novel, the changing content of dreams is designed to reflect an evolution of consciousness. At this point, Malreux seems close to an 'answer' or to fixing a perverted position, shown by the fact that these wholly death-driven dreams are hauntingly repetitive. Night terrors and daytime reality are shown to mingle confusingly for Malreux. The next time he goes ashore, his imagination is still filled with deathly images of the sea: 'Des idées formidables me tenaillaient le cerveau: faire la guerre à la mer, étrangler la mer, couper sa tête' (*TA* 234). The emotions of aggression and eroticized violence are mixed. The sea has become a dual signifier for the potential source of pleasure (dead women) and the eroticized object itself. The sea is boundless, deathly and traditionally feminine.

The association of sea and woman is brought to fatal fruition in the *acte pur* that Malreux commits while in a drunken stupor. He kills a prostitute with his knife, commenting afterwards: '— Ben, quoi? J'ai tué la mer!' (*TA* 238). Murder thus becomes the significant motif linking Barnabas and Malreux: on his deathbed, Barnabas will confess that the corpse he keeps in the cupboard is indeed his murdered wife.

All women (living and dead) become confused for Malreux, as he is unsure whether the murdered prostitute was not in fact his little Bretonne. This suggests a crime which attempts to remove the possibility of further prolongation of desire for an unattainable object. The true unattainable object is never of course to be found in another individual, but the creation of a talismanic corpse allows for the absence of fulfilment to have symbolic form. That these murders are born of desperate overreaching love is suggested by the words 'nous avions tué chacun une femme que nous aimions, étant ivres, ou d'amour ou de vin' (*TA* 253). The murdered woman becomes the original object, because she is henceforth unchanging, unchangeable and may be re-evoked in subsequent incarnations.

The denouement is both a demystification and a reinscription of the desirous structures instated in the text. Malreux is given access to the locked cupboard in order to bring the favoured object of desire to the dying Barnabas. Having embraced his talismanic head, Barnabas dies and Malreux throws the head into the sea. Barnabas and Malreux are presented in the closing pages of the novel in a father–son dialectic. Oedipal structures can be read in the action described. The son gains access to the object of desire (the father's love object and therefore the son's original lost object) and outlives patriarchal power. However, this is clearly a perverted version of Freud's model of familial desire, as Rachilde's aetiology of desire has necrophilic murder replacing the classic sexual content of the Oedipus complex.

The symbol of the severed female head, along with the collapsing of femininity onto the figure of the sea, suggests the presence of a fatal mother, a Medusa figure who symbolizes desire and death in one. Rachilde writes the masculine myth of the castrating woman into the text, but brings the question of death rather than that of castration to the surface. She achieves this by foregrounding repetitive images, ascribed to Malreux's unconscious, in which the notion of loss is given material form.

The overwhelming feelings of social and sexual alienation associated with Malreux are given ever more concrete form as the text moves towards its end. The lighthouse and the sea transmute from material realities into symbols of fragile male sexuality and an un-attainable other which threatens to overwhelm it. The impossiblity of 'strangling the sea' echoes the impossibility of achieving satiation in the stark emotional economy which Rachilde depicts. The ultimate trope is that of the dead body or dead part-object, which stand in for the nature of desire itself.

In *La Tour d'amour*, Rachilde demonstrates how necrophilia is the perfect figure with which to explore the workings of desire. Her tale of the coming-of-age of a necrophilic consciousness provides a struc-ture and image-base around which she weaves a convincing story of alienation and self-loss.

Vampirism as Desire: *Le Grand Saigneur*

La Tour d'amour represents, then, a unique high point in Rachilde's fiction. The fact that the setting is removed from the social or public sphere has allowed for the drama of individual consciousness and desire to take the privileged place. *Le Grand Saigneur* is a bizarre work which juxtaposes and collapses the realist setting of the social milieu of Parisian society with a subtext of myth, magic and superstition.

The poles of fantasy and realism seem to be personified by the two principal characters of the novel. The Saigneur/Seigneur of the title is Yves de Pontcroix, a mysterious aristocrat with a taste for blood and violence and an ancestral inheritance of vampirism. The female protagonist, Marie Faneau, is a struggling artist, a pragmatist whose work provides a foil for libidinal ambition. She is unaffected by desire, despite having already had a lover:

L'amour? Il lui a laissé un triste souvenir! S'est-elle donnée ou l'a-t-on prise? Elle a chassé l'intrus de son cœur et de ses bras. Un jour elle a appris qu'il était mort. Une paix profonde s'est abattue sur elle, non comme un deuil, mais comme une délivrance, et elle croit ne plus rien attendre en dehors des satisfactions que lui apporte son travail acharné.[18] (GS 32)

For Marie, the unsatisfactory aspect of sexuality lies in the realm of volition and agency; she is unsure whether she gave herself or was taken. Sexuality appears as something wholly ambiguous, whereas portraiture offers her a comforting dynamic of subject and object.

This theme of ambiguous desire is extended in the incestuous sibling bond which is implied between Marie and her brother Michel, who are orphans. Michel is a neurasthenic, neurotic and somewhat effeminate figure whose attachment to Marie is both anaclitic and erotic. She is 'à la fois le trésor qu'il admire, veut conserver pour lui seul et le trésorier dont il a un incessant besoin' (GS 29). Marie's relationship with Yves will shatter her preconceptions about desire and will also destroy her incestuous bond with her brother: Yves will eventually murder Michel to prevent him coming between them.

The symbolic language of the novel is somewhat heavy-handed. Yves woos Marie with gifts characterized by an almost humorous sombreness: red roses tied with a black ribbon, and pearls in a sinister black box. The engagement ring he will give her contains a blood-red ruby. While such obvious images may at first suggest a paucity of imagination, I would argue instead for a reading of this lack of subtlety as a deliberate attempt to draw mocking attention to recognizable conventions of romantic love.

Consider, for example, the moment when Marie's desire for Yves is awoken: 'Il y a toujours une heure où la fleur s'épanouit, inconsciente, que ce soit au soleil de midi ou au soleil de minuit, et le perce-neige aussi est une rose ...' (GS 74). The traditional flower imagery used to denote a young woman's sexual dawning is perhaps surprising in the context of Rachilde's usual more adventurous use of gender associations. Previously, we have seen males (Jacques and even Barnabas) likened to the symbols of delicate, doomed-to-fade beauty that are flowers. Here Marie is likened to a traditional image of womanliness. However, I would suggest that this has less to do with her sex per se than with the role she will play in her sexual dialectic with Yves. Throughout her work, Rachilde manipulates the traditional associations of flowers—passivity, beauty—but they are no longer synonymous with the female sex, or even with femininity. Rather, the symbolic presence of flowers indicates only the identity of (willing) victim. A flower that has been picked is a kind of living corpse. Marie's progressive assumption of the position of victim will be reinforced throughout the text by the numerous mentions of (red) flowers that Yves will send her.

The development of Marie and Yves's emotional liaison is described in terms which suggest a difference from 'normal' courtship but also a close parodying of it, a perverse or ironic paralleling exemplified in the incident recounted as follows: 'Il lui baisa les mains, appuyant à peine, selon la formule, puis il garda ses poignets, un instant, en les serrant d'une manière intolérable' (GS 79–80). The conventions of romantic love are called to our attention here. They are maintained and indeed explicitly referred to ('selon la formule'), but the undertones of violence and possession always present beneath courtly love are immediately visible.

Yet, as well as demystifying existing conventions, Rachilde injects some of her own mystery into her presentation of this bizarre romance. Pontcroix's violence is presented as something more than the aggression which is commonly associated with masculinity: 'Je suis très violent ... pas dans le mauvais sens du mot. Je suis incapable de vous offenser ... à la manière des hommes ordinaires' (GS 80). In place of the ambiguity of incestuous desire or of female equivocation in the face of sexual surrender, we have a different level of ambiguity: that of defining the manifestation of Yves's desire. What exactly would it mean to be violent in a good way? Or to cause harm in the manner of an extraordinary man? The *points de suspension*, which are used to suggest mystery or the unsayable many times in Rachilde's work, are once again brought into service.

Consider the following declaration on Yves's part: 'Vous me plaisez tellement que je cherche le mot qui doit vous faire comprendre ce que je ressens pour vous ... mais un autre mot ... que celui qu'on prononce toujours en pareille circonstance, ce mot qui ne signifie rien et qui a la prétension de résumer tout' (GS 84). The question is raised: just what emotion and act would this ideal partnership lead to? A note of un-fathomability is injected into the textual representations of love by Yves's hinting at an unnameable formula that would render them unified. The word 'love' is brought to our attention here by the very fact of its absence. In this expression it has only a negative value, an incapacity to signify in the language of Pointcroix's violent excess of desire.

Soon this game of inadequate signifiers and eloquent silences finds a voice in the replacement of the word 'amour' with another. Yves's proposal of marriage is enacted in the following, quirky formula: 'En devenant mienne, ma femme légitime, comme je l'entends, désormais, vous ne risquez que la mort ... Acceptez-vous?' (GS 104). At these surprising words, Marie has a strong reaction, almost fainting with shock: 'cet homme n'avait donc pas de cœur qu'il remplaçait le mot *amour* par le mot *mort*?' (104). The literal lexical substitution of death for love here enacts an eruption at the textual surface of the underlying conceit in the treatment of desire. This is a disruption engineered consciously by the author, who places the revealing word in the mouth of one of her characters expressly to draw attention to her literary aims.

Consider: 'Marie, je désire votre vie, votre sang, votre admirable santé, votre adorable beauté' (GS 105). Sexual desire is de-metaphorized and revealed as the approach to death, but this is re-metaphorized as belonging locally to the genre of the vampire tale in the above quotation and in the pun in the title.

In a moment of *petite mort*, which is much less metaphorical than the traditional orgasm, Marie faints in a confused transport. This is firstly because Yves has squeezed her hands until they are blue, and secondly because a transformation has been wrought in her desiring consciousness. On recovering, Marie seems convinced of her emotional affinity with Yves: '— Oui, je veux être sa femme. Je le veux. Après tout ... je ne risque rien ... La mort, mais, c'est une plaisanterie, la mort, en amour ...' (*GS* 108). This represents a moment of transition. The two signifiers of 'love' and 'death' are linked for Marie, and the novel can now digress by examining ways of encoding and representing this associated idea. This is attempted through a discussion of the various strands of the vampire myth.

The idea of text within text is explored in the novel's two central chapters. Chapter 6 narrates the evening of the engagement cele-brations, in which storytelling plays an important role. Yves and his close friend, Dr Duhat, recount the legend of Pontcroix's ancestral haunted tower: 'Il s'agissait, je crois, d'une femme infidèle qui fut condamnée, par un de mes ancêtres, à mourir de faim' (*GS* 127). The motifs of marital love, power and death are woven into the retelling of the legend, sounding a note of warning to Marie. Note the libidinal nature of the details of the bride's demise at the fangs of her husband's vampire, who visits her tower in the form of a bird: 'Les grandes ailes mouvantes, à grands coups d'éventail, bercèrent l'agonie de la belle condamnée pendant que l'amoureux bourreau, le bec enfoui dans sa poitrine, lui buvait le sang jusqu'au cœur' (*GS* 132). The oxymoronic ideas of 'bercèrent l'agonie' and 'amoureux bourreau', mixing tenderness and brutality, are reminiscent of the language of Baudelaire. Moreover, the insertion of the vampire legend into the text, in the mouth of Yves, has the effect of articulating, through well-known allegorical means, a version of the desire which he wants to communicate to Marie. This also suggests to the contemporary French reader a link with the Gothic tradition and the vampire tale with which they are familiar, exemplified by the tales of Hoffmann and Gautier's 'La Morte amoureuse'.

Having introduced the figure of the vampire into the field of storytelling, Yves acts upon this idea in his goodnight kiss to Marie: '[Le] marquis de Pontcroix se pencha sur son cou; là, derrière l'oreille rose, sur cette chair fine comme les pétales des fleurs de la corbeille, il mit les lèvres et, sous le baiser brutal, odieux, le sang jaillit, deux gouttelettes pourpres de l'exacte nuance du rubis de la bague des fiançailles' (*GS* 136). The heavy insistence on the link between pain and marriage, given in the simile above (where the engagement ring and blood are linked), suggests that *Le Grand Saigneur* could be a pastiche or critique of courtship and marriage. The husband as vampire is a seductive rhetorical figure for social critique, and indeed, we must not underplay the importance of this idea as a potential interpretation of the novel. Yet we cannot ignore, either, the fact that

RACHILDE AND THE DEATH OF GENDER   113

questions of desire are privileged throughout the text, in such a way as to suggest that Rachilde's conceit looks beyond the issue of social organization. However, these two readings are not mutually exclusive. The fact that society organizes desire around the institution of marriage means that an interpretation on this level may support or elucidate my own approach.

Michel's commentary on the bloody kiss draws together both of the threads discussed above: '— Au revoir, marquis ... de Sade! gronda Michel' (GS 137). The linking of Yves with the archetypal aristocratic sadist suggests both the corruption of social privilege and the immediate association of perverse desire and pathological cruelty. It adds to the insistence upon intertextuality which characterizes this central section of the novel.

The intertextual, interdiscursive play is foregrounded in Chapter 8, which leaves aside the story of Yves and Marie, to present a history of the vampire legend and a pseudo-scientific treatment of it. It details local historical theories of the origin of the vampire (couplings between humans and animals, the restless corpses of those possessed of too large an appetite) and it places two authorities on the vampire side by side. Firstly, there are long passages from the work of Augustin Calmet (1672–1757).[19] Rachilde quotes his definition of the vampire: 'Mort qui sort de son tombeau, spécialement la nuit, pour tourmenter les vivants, le plus souvent en les suçant au cou et d'autres fois en leur serrant la gorge au point de les étouffer' (GS 144). Calmet, then, supports the supernatural explanation of the vampire as found in the unscientific discourse of mythology and superstition. Secondly, Rachilde offers the following comment as a kind of demystifying afterword to the four pages of quotations from Calmet: 'On a connu des malades, doués d'une imagination trop vive, qui, frappés par une violente commotion cérébrale, ne concevaient plus l'acte d'amour que sous l'empire de l'idée fixe de voir couler du sang et devenaient des sadiques, malgré leur propension à la plus romanesques des pudeurs' (GS 149). We might remember that prior to the naming of 'necrophilia' in 1861, 'vampirism' was the offence for which the violators of tombs and corpses, such as Sergeant Bertrand, were prosecuted. Thus, two discourses on the vampire are contained in this central chapter: on the one hand that of legend, incorporating theories of the supernatural, and on the other, that of contemporary Western science, as suggested by the terminology 'malades' and 'commotion cérébrale'. The pathologizing and taxonomizing prose of

Krafft–Ebing is echoed here, replacing the supernatural being with the modern sexual pervert.

We may again be reminded of Dauphiné's assertion that Rachilde's works should be read as 'l'illustration littéraire de manuels de psychopathologie sexuelle'. Yet in their self-awareness they are clearly more than that. Here, Rachilde is explicitly playing with this idea, suggesting perhaps that the writer may sometimes take on the voice of the scientist and pass comment on her own creation.[20] In the context of this isolated section of the work, this suggests a meta–text in which the primary artistic content of the novel and incorporated voice of 'authority' are held up as alternative fictions or alternative reading strategies. The perspective of medicine continues in the text in the voice of Dr Duhat, who will later describe Yves as a 'cas de clinique' (*GS* 239) and talk of his condition in terms that clearly suggest psychopathy: 'Il n'était pas fou, seulement privé de sensibilité' (256).

In naming the figure of the vampire, Rachilde harnesses a mythic figure that allows us, through its rich associative history, an unspoken understanding of the dark stirrings of desire. By contrast, she shows us time and again that the characters themselves are unable to speak their desire. Consider Yves's words: 'Ah! Je ne veux pas vous faire du mal ... ne me tentez pas! Tout l'amour ou rien! Ça ne me suffirait pas, votre amour à vous. C'est trop peu' (*GS* 233). Here we see the rather confusing articulation of a wish to 'go all the way': 'Tout l'amour ou rien'. Precisely what is Yves talking about? I would suggest that this ultimate manifestation of desire is neither sexual intercourse nor actual murder: it is some impossible annihilation which prolongs life within death—the sort of impossible act we have been chasing through the century's literary production. The figure of vampirism is perhaps as close as one can get to representing this shadowy idea of a death–driven passion which allows for both the passage into death and the survival of the victim, so that the death can be acted out again and again on the other. It is the underlying fantasy of necrophilia.

We are repeatedly presented in the text with two possible understandings of Yves de Pontcroix's position. Perhaps he is an undead vampire coming of a long and noble race of vampires. Or, as Dr Duhat puts it, he is a *cas de clinique* because he fails to understand the social principle that 'l'amour, c'est ce qui donne la vie, ce n'est pas ce qui tue' (*GS* 239). But our reading thus far authorizes a third option: that Marie and Yves are embodiments of a structural principle of desire. They represent a desire which wants more than it can achieve in corporeal sexual form, which takes the spark of a long-buried atavistic drive for destruction as its source, and which seeks out the beyond of absence in the realm of the other.

Consider Yves's words regarding the marital prescription, sexual intercourse: 'Et cela, pour quelques secondes de plaisir vraiment inférieur dont je ne pourrais pas me contenter, moi, dont la puissance réside dans le cerveau, c'est-à-dire est illimitée' (*GS* 239) and later 'mon amour, à moi, est d'une essence un peu plus rare que celui des humains, parce qu'il ne finit pas. La satiété ne le menace pas. Il n'a pas le but ridicule de la procréation' (270). There is a strong tone of arrogance and superiority here. If we want to take a pathologizing view of the character, we can read Yves as the exemplary pervert having found his 'preferable' resolution to the problematic of lack in desire. Sexual intercourse is unsatisfactory because it is terminable and because the union of the two is potentially interrupted by a child, a third term.

At certain moments, the text has been concerned with de-metaphorizing desire and re-encoding it according to genre or discourse. The difficulty of the denouement lies in knowing where the metaphor and de-metaphorization begin and end. As Marie and Pontcroix are driven to their honeymoon destination of the ancestral castle, the wedding night has become a dreaded object of mystery and fear for Marie. In the marital bedroom, the confusion regarding what may happen to cement their desire for and beyond death escalates. Yves proposes that he has the right to exchange the husband's traditional wedding-night privilege for a consummation that would be more to his taste: 'rendez-moi cette justice, c'est que j'ai le droit pour moi. Sang pour sang! J'ai le plein pouvoir de l'époux qui réclame celui d'une virginité' (*GS* 273). Here deflowering is used as a metaphor for what he wants to do to her, in a bold reversal of the usual metaphorical equivalence which has death as a metaphor for sex. Yet Yves does not kill Marie, and Marie does not give in to his passion for slow blood-letting. A sort of stalemate is reached. That, in some ways, the experiment with desire in the novel becomes a structural impasse is suggested by the final narrative event: Yves's suicide.

This ending is rather unexpected and unconvincing in an otherwise complex novel. Yves's suicide is a semantic puzzle. Read as the sole course of action open to Yves other than making Marie into a vampire, it can be seen as an eternal deferral of desire. The final words of the novel, which are accorded to Dr Duhat, say as much: '— Si elle peut croire cela, et c'est possible, elle l'aimera toujours. Il vient de recréer *le vampire*' (GS 279). By giving Duhat the last word, and by removing the conceit of Yves's supernatural vampiric immortality through his death, Rachilde may be seen to come down on the side of science, or rather of a rational explanation of desire. The image of creating a new vampire suggests a figure for ongoing, insatiable desire: Marie will not have him, nor will she have her death at his hands. This suggests, on a libidinal level, a vampire-like state of eternal un-satisfaction.

The figure of the vampire in this novel represents a metaphysical experiment with death. The vampire, as 'undead', is neither fully dead nor really alive; he is a corpse, and yet animate: an embodiment of paradox and tension. The relationship between Marie and Yves shows up the complex and surprising truth of the dynamic of necrophilia. At one point Marie comments: 'je m'imagine que cet homme *est mort*' (GS 154). It is Marie who is the necrophile, despite the portrayal of Yves as predatory and obsessed with death. Her desire for a man who she imagines is dead, and who, at the same time, she thinks will kill her, suggests a narrative acting out of the wishful identificatory fantasy underlying necrophilia. One interpretation of the novel is that Yves is no more than the projection of Marie's unconscious desire. The impossible corpse that Yves embodies is the ideal, exquisite corpse of necrophilic fantasy.

Some Concluding Remarks

Rachilde's novels play with stereotypes and clichés of love and sexuality in the interest of shattering received ideas and radically challenging norms. This is achieved not so much by playing with social expectations of gender and sex in the novels, but by challenging the traditions of generic form. Rachilde perverts the conventions of the realist love story by recasting the romantic hero as a vampire and a man's first love as a murdered corpse. In each case, Rachilde's self-deconstructing narratives and myths demonstrate the desire for death that subtends human coupling and goes beyond the 'rational' sadomasochistic dynamic.

The fact that Rachilde reworked the theme of impossible desire many times over three quarters of a century suggests an inevitable frustration with the attempt to embody desire in words. However, we have seen that she abandoned fairly early on in her career the game of gendered pronoun-swapping which so many consider her major artistic and political statement. We can posit that by the time of writing *La Tour d'amour* and *Le Grand Saigneur*, Rachilde felt that less obvious textual work on the level of gender presentation needed to be performed in order to show up the dialectic of death-driven desire at work.

From her male contemporaries, such as Barrès, to recent feminist readers, few have known quite what to make of Rachilde. The tendency to pathologize her has never gone away completely. Renée A. Kingcaid, noting the presence of sexuality and death drive in Rachilde's work, claims that she exhibits 'the ultimate symptom of the neurotic repulsion-attraction complex of feminine sexuality [...] the conviction that sex and death are one'.[21] The mention of neurosis here echoes Barrès's description of Rachilde's 'fatigue nerveuse' with which I opened this chapter. It seems that while nineteenth-century men were afraid of female creativity, some twentieth-century feminists may well be wary of female expressions of alternative and non-reproductive sexual desire. Moreover, to envisage the psychical link between sex and death as a local expression of Rachilde's neurotic desire is intrinsically to cut short our understanding. If this idea appears with such pervasive insistence through literature and cultural production of the nineteenth century, it is at the very least a mass or universal neurosis. It is by entering into the rhetoric of the texts that we may reach a more thorough understanding of the concept.

One theory to account for Rachilde's cold critical reception until recently is that in order to extract what is particularly complex from her work, we need a paradigm of reading that can interact with her own agenda as a writer. While the bias of psychoanalytic and deconstructive criticism tends to be one of knowing better than the writer, in the case of Rachilde, a careful look at her production on its own literal terms is particularly profitable. Such contemporary critical currents as gender and queer theory are conceptual tools that can be usefully placed into dialogue with Rachilde's texts. I have indicated above a few examples where Rachilde's collapsing of gender and sexuality as meaningful categories directly prefigures the radical philosophy of Judith Butler. More research needs to be done on the experimental treatment of desire by *fin-de-siècle* writers, particularly Rachilde, as precursors of postmodern theories of sexuality popularized in the 1980s and 90s. My present analysis of the necrophilic imagination in literature contributes to this broader project.

I hope to have shown that it is the key with which we can unlock much of what is most daring and rich in Rachilde's work.

Notes to Chapter 4

1. Maurice Barrès, preface to Rachilde, *Monsieur Vénus* (Paris: Flammarion, 1926), p. xx.
2. Ibid.
3. Jennifer Birkett, *The Sins of the Fathers* (London: Quartet, 1986).
4. Diana Holmes, 'Rachilde, decadence, misogyny and the woman writer', in *French Women's Writing 1848–1994* (London: Athlone Press, 1996), 63–82, and *Rachilde: Decadence, Gender and the Woman Writer* (Oxford: Berg, 2001).
5. Alison Finch, 'Rachilde and the horror of gender confusion', in *Women's Writing in Nineteenth-Century France* (Cambridge: Cambridge University Press, 2000), 206–17.
6. Birkett, *Sins of the Fathers*, 161.
7. Holmes, *Rachilde*, 4.
8. *La Marquise de Sade* [1887] (Paris: Gallimard, 1996), 214.
9. Claude Dauphiné, *Rachilde* (Paris: Mercure de France, 1991), 53.
10. It was Rachilde's own favourite of all her novels. Laurent Tailhade called it her 'chef-d'œuvre', according to Claude Dauphiné who shares Tailhade's opinion of the novel's quality. See Dauphiné, *Rachilde*, 96.
11. *Monsieur Vénus* [1884] (Paris: Flammarion, 1926) [*MV*], 46.
12. It should be noted that this attempt to do away with 'sexist language' can be seen to prefigure directly Monique Wittig's *Gedankenexperiment* in *Les Guérillères* (1969) to create a subject of language which is a generic plural pronoun incorporating both male and female. In the post-patriarchal utopia she creates, human subjects no longer signify as 'men' and 'women'; gender itself has become redundant.
13. Ironically, at Rachilde's trial for obscenity, the *ministre public* indeed accused her of having 'inventé un vice de plus' (see Dauphiné, *Rachilde*, 56).
14. Judith Butler, 'Imitation and gender insubordination' [1991], in *The Lesbian and Gay Studies Reader*, ed. Henry Abelove, Michèle Aina Barale and David M. Halperin (London: Routledge, 1993), 307–20 (315).
15. I am thinking of Freud's description of 'an average uncultivated woman in whom the same polymorphously perverse disposition persists', with which feminists have since taken issue: 'If she is led on by a clever seducer she will find every sort of perversion to her taste, and will retain them as part of her own sexual activities' (*SE* vii. 191).
16. Dauphiné, *Rachilde*, 319.
17. *La Tour d'amour* [1899] (Paris: Les Maîtres du Livre, 1916) [*TA*], 28–9.
18. *Le Grand Saigneur* (Paris: Flammarion, 1922) [*GS*], 32.
19. A theologian and expert on the occult, remembered for *Dissertations sur les apparitions des anges, des démons et des esprits et sur les revenants et vampires de Hongrie, de Bohème, de Moravie et de Silésie* (1750).
20. It should be noted that this technique of incorporating scientific and sociological discourses into the body of works of art is very much a part of the *fin-de-siècle*

fashion. Other examples include Flaubert's *Bouvard et Pécuchet* (1881), which plays on the idea of the generic form of the anatomy; Zola's *Rougon-Macquart* cycle (1871–93), which consistently personifies the voices of art and science, and Huysmans's *Là-bas* (1891), which incorporates the (fictional) biography of the paedophilic mass-murderer Gilles de Rais.

21. Renée A. Kingcaid, *Neurosis as Narrative: The Decadent Fiction of Proust, Lorrain, and Rachilde* (Carbondale: Southern Illinois University Press, 1992), 17.

CONCLUSION

L'étrange mot d'urbanisme, qu'il vienne d'un pape Urbain ou de la Ville, il ne se préoccupera peut-être plus des morts. Les vivants se débarrasseront des cadavres, sournoisement ou non, comme on se défait d'une pensée honteuse. En les expédiant au four crématoire, le monde urbanisé se défera d'un grand secours théâtral, et peut-être du théâtre. À la place du cimetière, centre — peut-être excentré — de la ville, vous aurez des columbariums, avec cheminée, sans cheminée, avec ou sans fumée, et les morts, calcinés comme des petits pains calcinés, serviront d'engrains pour les kolkhozes ou les kibboutzim, assez loin de la ville.

JEAN GENET[1]

In this comment on the anthropology of modernity, Jean Genet points out that the processes of urbanization bring with them an alienating sanitization of the human relationship with death. The signs of death are no longer allowed to occupy centre-stage in our social space or in the late-modern consciousness. The crematorium, built on the edge of town, announces with its eradicating flames the disappearance of the celebratory, symbolic rite of passage of the body entering death. Genet links the role of the death ritual intimately with the role of art, such that relegating signs of death to the limits of perception is equal to a silencing of the artist and the death of theatre.

This passage, then, sounds a note of warning. It suggests that the only thing more deadly than death itself is an arrogant denial of death's empire. Like theatre with its cathartic function, rituals and reminders of death have served historically both as a vanitas and as a communal spur to emotion and self-reflection. A society which refuses symbolization of the passing of generations is an alienated society; reduced to the immediate moment; steeped in a solipsistic functionality. Genet's dystopia is, perhaps, a social space much like today's Western society.

In Chapter 1, I examined the French nineteenth century as a cultural epoch in which death was symbolized almost to excess. The traumatic fluctuations of early modernity can be read to produce a reactive profusion of images of death, signifying a comforting permanence in the face of relativizing cultural transition. In the figure of necrophilia, the notion of death—through the jointly material and ideational symbol of death that is the corpse—is made conscious as an object of desire and identification. For the late nineteenth-century consciousness, characterized by the death of God, the rise of the individual, and the birth of the psychoanalytic subject, such representational strategies may be read as attempts to thematize the workings of desire itself.

In the early twenty-first century, we have seen a move from modern to postmodern consciousness. As the subject is decentred, deconstructed and pluralized, we may ask what happens to the spectres of desire evoked in previous centuries. What is the meaning of necrophilia today, and has it any relevance beyond the Romantic and Decadent conventions which embraced it?

This conclusion is in three parts. Firstly, it will briefly reprise the implications of my reading of necrophilia for an understanding of nineteenth-century literary and aesthetic criticism. Secondly, it will undertake a discussion of the way in which this project impacts upon recent theories of gender and sexuality. Thirdly, it will return to the question posed above by means of a discussion of the legacy of necrophilia in the twentieth and early twenty-first centuries.

Necrophilia and Aesthetics

One must be cautious of making any grand claim for an intrinsic or ahistorical a priori link between death-driven desire and the pro-duction of literature. However, in readings of specific texts, it has been possible to show that certain structures of psychical desire and certain aesthetic techniques are closely aligned and operate in a mimetic relation. In Baudelaire's verse and in his critical prose, the same libidinal economy was seen to be at work, although operating differently within the strictures of different generic conventions. Baudelaire's art criticism is an interface between the expression of desire and the discussion of aesthetics. Certain of the wider implications of this idea can be developed.

The idea that creativity operates as a process of transformation between psychical fantasy and textual object in the world is a persuasive one. Transformation is a keyword in debates regarding aesthetics for such figures as Baudelaire, and its roots can be traced back to classical authors. In Ovid's *Metamorphoses*, transformation is intimately linked to sexuality. Gods, aroused by the beauty of mortals, transformed themselves into beasts or mythical creatures in order to consummate their desire. Conversely, those guilty of too much or of inappropriate desire were subject to a punishing change of form. As well as being linked to sexuality, transformation is associated with death. The predominance of the theme of metamorphosis in mythology can be partly explained by the primitive belief that the human spirit of the dead can pass into the body of another being or of an animal. The concept of the totemic animal and the rites created around it by primitive societies have been treated by Frazer's canonical text of anthropology and by Freud's late work on the origins of religion.[2]

In the literary texts under study, transformation has been seen on many different levels. In an extension of his conscious project of transforming mud into gold, Baudelaire is a libidinal alchemist throughout his production. Poems such as 'À une Madone' and 'Une martyre' reveal a poetic play of fluidity and fixity, intimately inter-woven with images of murder and destruction. His art criticism performs transformative elevation of the work of others by appropriating and fixing the object in Baudelairean interpretation. These dramas are mapped onto verse and prose which mirror the psychical structures of necrophilic fixing and possessing. An analysis of Rachilde's novels showed that textual games to do with transforming gender and gender-meaning are ultimately in the service of suspending such differences and showing up a dialectic of destruction.

At the level of writerly work, then, it is clear that, in each case, the trope of transformation works as a device for suggesting artistic or imaginative innovation. Yet the presence of perverse thematic material suggests that the transformation at work runs much deeper than the textual surface. Just as the primitive mind understands meta-morphosis as the regeneration of the spirit in a new body, so textual necrophilic transformations involve a dynamic of resurrection. A Freudian reading would understand this in terms of archaic (infantile) desirous structures transposed into representational forms: the relics of the pre-linguistic washed up on the shores of the social.

For Freud, the transformation of the sexual instinct is the key to understanding adult perversion:

It is perhaps in connection precisely with the most repulsive perversions that the mental factor must be regarded as playing its largest part in the transformation of sexual instinct [...] In their case a piece of mental work has been performed which [...] is the equivalent of an idealization of the instinct. The omnipotence of love is perhaps never more strongly proved than in such aberrations as these. (*Three Essays on the Theory of Sexuality* (1), *SE* vii. 161)

Joining the mental model to the artistic imaginary, Freud's words could be used to explain the very process by which rebarbative material becomes art. When an artist chooses to work with a particular type of material that appears initially disturbing or disgusting, s/he is entering into a conscious project of idealizing transformation. We have noticed time and again how the writers in question posit fixity and deathliness as the most beautiful sort of transforming gesture they can make to their objects. Artistic or textual, as well as mental, work idealizes the subject matter and makes the representation as beautiful as possible. This may be one understanding of what is meant by the notion of artistic transformation.

However, such a one-way process of transformation, in the direction of unequivocal beauty, is not wholly consistent with the necrophilic texts discussed. In the case of 'Une martyre', artistic success comes in the perfect mapping of subject matter onto form, but reading this poem is not a 'pleasant' experience, and the *jouissance* it produces is as much an experience of shock as one of pleasure. More precisely, it is a reaction of shock at the seductive means by which the scenario is embodied in language, even as an element of distaste lingers. The aggravations of disgust, putrescence and obscenity are actively sought and, despite their apparent sublimation into high art, something is left over of their uncanny ability to disturb. We have seen that Freud's theory of the death drive adds a complexity to the concept of the pleasure principle and attempts to account for the previously unfathomable human tendency in the direction of self-sabotage and destruction. So it is that death drive acts as a metaphor for certain types of writerly practice that reveal an excess of the desire to represent beyond what is beautiful.

In Baudelaire's case, the myth of a Christ-figure is rewritten in a poem evoking a sexualized female sacrifice. In Rachilde's *Le Grand Saigneur*, the vampire myth is updated and used as a figure for the underpinnings of death-driven perversion. This can be read as the archaic transforming into the modern: superstitious myth recast in the language of sexology. What is done thematically in terms of transformative work is symptomatic of what happens at the level of fantasy also. In Baudelaire's and Rachilde's texts, the desire leading to the threat of castration is systematically removed and the desire or threat of death at the hands of another put in its place. Thus, a central Freudian myth is unwritten, and an alternative founding myth established, which has the ultimate self-loss of death as its origin.

If a theory of aesthetics is capable of presenting a mirror to the psyche, as we assume a work of art to be, this cannot operate only on the level of an individual writer's subjectivity. Such a relation may be heavily historically dependent and may reveal insights into a local group. A particular set of aesthetic theories, adhered to at a particular moment in literary history, must indicate a mass concern or shared cultural fantasy. Art and literature clearly do not inhabit a pure, non-social realm, even when the credo of the time (for example Parnassianism) states that they should. Theory-making about art is one of the principal tools that a culture has for interpreting and suggesting meaning. In Chapter 3, it was proposed that Baudelaire's critical writing was part of a continuum of narcissistic, death-driven production, rather than an aloof and objective assessment. Here, I am suggesting that aesthetic theory may always be narcissistic or, as a Lacanian would have it, characterized by an Imaginary relation (one of wishful identification in which the world is understood by reference to the self). In the case of these writers, the fashion for dead objects is anything but coincidental and betrays method or process as much as a choice of subject matter.

Gender and Sexual Politics

One concern expressed by previous critical investigations of the necrophilic imagination in culture, particularly Elisabeth Bronfen's study, is that this apparently objectifying perversion is intrinsically misogynistic. The social reality of male power, as well as stereotypes regarding male aggression and female passivity, mean that more often than not, men are figured as violent agents and women as their victims. The taxonomical construction of mass-murder as a socio-legal phenomenon came about in the mid-nineteenth century, with the crimes of Jack the Ripper. Since then, the archetypal perpetrator in reality and fiction has been male. Cameron and Frazer (1987) argue that this is because sexual intercourse, with its clear biological poles of penetrator and recipient, is the paradigm upon which all socially encoded models of desire, however perverse, are based. For them, murder and necrophilia are exaggerated manifestations of 'ordinary' masculinity in a continuum of desire.

I have sketched throughout this book the skeletal model for an aetiology of desire which locates primary and genderless auto-destructive urges as the original source of desire. However, we cannot ignore the fact that society controls and makes meaning out of desire by inscribing sexual difference on psyches and bodies, and by attributing significance to 'masculinity' and 'femininity'. Although we may now possess the critical apparatus with which to deconstruct these meanings, it is difficult to think outside them, as they are an intrinsic part of our social conditioning and form the basis of our understanding of identity.

Nineteenth-century literature, particularly in France, is replete with examples of sexual confusion. This is perhaps best seen in Balzac's 'Sarrasine', which undermines the notion of phallic power by making the castrated male the object of desire. This tale could almost be a Lacanian parable *avant la lettre*, as the object of desire is a 'man' whom the protagonist takes to be a 'woman'. Yet he is a 'man' who is robbed of the very thing which determines him socially (his relation to the phallus). He is displaced from his link in the signifying chain, always already pregnant with absence and loss. In this way he is desocialized. Similarly, the figure of the androgyne is a favourite in nineteenth-century literature. Gautier's poem 'Contralto' plays succinctly on the suspension of absolutes that is the essence of the not-man, not-woman:

> On voit dans le musée antique,
> Sur un lit de marbre sculpté
> Une statue énigmatique
> D'une inquiétante beauté.
>
> Est-ce un jeune homme? est-ce une femme,
> Une déesse, ou bien un dieu?
> L'amour, ayant peur d'être infâme,
> Hésite et suspend son aveu. (*Œuvres complètes*, ii. 31)

I have been arguing that the division of gender is an arbitrary complication in the field of originally undifferentiated desire. Writing such as this is disruptive in so far as it blurs the absolute lines of distinction separating masculine and feminine, male and female. It thereby challenges the social system of meaning-making. While literature is clearly part of social discourse, it is also capable of suspending social realities in favour of imaginative fantasy. To use a Lacanian model, literature and art intersect the Symbolic and the Imaginary and, at the moments of highest expression, may even allow partial access to the Real.

I am aware, however, of a very valid objection to this argument. Nineteenth-century games of gender confusion and gender inversion (such as are favoured by Rachilde) do not necessarily preclude misogyny, as they can be seen to show contempt for 'the feminine'. When the very masculine Raoule has the very feminine Jacques killed, is this not a misogynist act, just another murder of the feminine? If representations repeatedly show the feminine as the object of sacrifice, what position is left for that class of person (women) allotted the role of femininity by society? Following this logic, women may have no choice but to identify erotically with the readily available representations of themselves as victims. Feminists, beginning with Simone de Beauvoir, have talked of this socially acquired female masochism in terms of identification with the oppressor or the existential concept of bad faith.[3]

As I have stated, I am aware of the persuasiveness of such an argument. However, Freud's model, which holds that both sexes face a death-driven relation to self and other, only later mediated by society and channelled into different aims, can be helpful if we wish to avoiding thinking in terms of the inevitability of male agency and female passivity. In this model, primary masochism or the desire to experience victimhood would be the obvious strategic resort of desire. Throughout my analysis, I have wanted not only to separate masculinity from maleness, femininity from femaleness, but to do away with, or more accurately to suspend, 'masculinity' and 'femininity' as names for modes or positions of desirous behaviour and fantasy implying activity or passivity. The adoption of the terms doer/done-to, necrophile/corpse etc. has been partly in the interests of loosening these positions from the notion of sexed subjects and even from notions of socially constructed gender. Activity and passivity have been remapped onto a landscape of death-driven desire, which operates according to a logic of shifting projections and identifications, in which their absolute meanings become uncertain.

Art which were purely Imaginary would not be very good art. But equally, art located completely in the Symbolic would be a dry and discursive entity indeed. Good art allows us privileged access to the ways in which the phantasmal and the imaginative realms bisect and are effected by the so-called real world. While remaining aware of the social, such writings retain a glimpse of the intangible, the relics of infantile phantasy, the echo of the primal encounter with the abyss. And as we distance ourselves from the social in this way, we may simultaneously get a clearer view of it. A reading which strategically suspends questions of gender may, in fact, show up precisely the underlying formulations to which straightforward inquiries are too close. By entering the critical sphere at the imaginary level on which the texts themselves are operating, a unique insight into desire presents itself. I would suggest that the terms 'masculine' and 'feminine' fit badly the roles of 'doer' and 'done-to', but that they have come to wear them because the metaphor of gender is the means by which desire is translated into the world and into language. The next stage in this process of metaphorical translation is that of 'masculine' and 'feminine' onto 'man' and 'woman', a more obvious misfit which has already been demystified by Butler and others.

Imaginary constructs of necrophilic desire, which reveal the aim of transgressing the boundaries between life and death, self and other, rather than achieving a particular gendered configuration, para-doxically provide insight into the workings of a gendered society. They do this by denaturalizing the social rhetoric which has the male–female, masculine–feminine pairs as the default and absolute model of duality.

On the one hand, a focus upon the death-seeking nature of desire, and particularly upon the death-giving nature of intersubjective desire, may seem a morbid, disturbing or negative current in human subjectivity and in the creative act. Indeed, in his *Death, Desire and Loss in Western Culture*, Jonathan Dollimore concludes by attempting to distinguish a paradigm of desire, located in gay writing, which would steer away from the destructive, lack-propelled model that has clouded Western thought.[4] Yet I would like to propose that an understanding of human desire which takes into account our attraction towards destruction can in some ways be a liberating understanding. The necrophile's relation to the corpse describes a relation to her/himself as much as to the other. The dialectic of difference is broken by the third term—which is the idea of omnipresent, intangible and ungendered death itself. In its aesthetic incarnations, this destructive passion offers desirous positions that are as free-floating and liberating as one can hope to find.

Aftermath

The establishment of the perversions as medical classifications in the nineteenth century marks the first—however ideologically problematic—acknowledgement by a secular authority of the diversity and plurality of sexual desire. What Sade's *Les Cent-vingt Journées de Sodome* has attempted to do in the sphere of pornographic writing, sexology does in the service of knowledge and societal control. The further we move from ideas of what is 'natural' in sexual desire and behaviour, the more autonomous we may seem to become as desiring beings. Individual control of fertility by means of contraception and abortion, and the (partial) social acceptance of homosexuality as a lifestyle, effect a conscious dissociation of pleasure and procreation in the Western world. The postmodern subject is no longer indoctrinated with the imperative to reproduce. Desire can be harnessed purely in the service of self-gratification and self-exploration. The idea that sex has a fundamental relationship with making babies has become an archaism, thanks to the ubiquity of discourses of free sexual expression and the increasing displacement of the reproductive function onto the turkey baster and the test tube.

It would be impossible to assert that the literature of nineteenth-century France can be read as a direct point of origin for subsequent representations of unusual desire. However, as I have demonstrated above, the nineteenth century certainly marks a turning point in the conceptualization of sexuality and subjectivity. Twentieth-century artistic representations of the desire for the dead operate in ways that are both different from, and yet retain traces of, the mechanisms seen in the nineteenth-century works discussed. I have noticed three principal tendencies in such contemporary works.

Firstly, a group of texts exists which take as their focus the figure of a 'real-life' necrophile around whom they craft postmodern myths. The exploits of Sergeant Bertrand were the inspiration for two twentieth-century novels: Guy de Wargny's *La Bête noire* (1965) and Guy Endore's *Le Loup-Garou de Paris* (1987). Similarly, the British necrophiliac serial killers John Christie and Dennis Nilsen have been the inspiration for several recent works of art and literature.[5] This strand of representation instates the death-driven subject as the logical hero of a radically individuated society. This suggests that contemporary aesthetic trends lie along a continuum with, and yet also represent a break from, long-standing traditions. The heroic necrophilic murderer is an echo of the criminal hero of Frenetic Romanticism, reminding us of Gautier's poetic celebration of Lacenaire's crimes. The late twentieth-century cult of 'serial-killer chic' can also, however, be seen as a symptom of an apparently ethically dead culture, in which multimedia saturation leaves a reading and viewing public anaesthetized to all but the most extreme images.

The second strand of necrophilic representation in postmodern culture is marked by a personalization of sexual experience and a tendency to focus on 'deviation' as a self-chosen badge of identity. Social and legal attitudes towards necrophilia have not changed to the extent of endorsing the perpetration of sexual relations with corpses and, to my knowledge, no 'necrophile liberation movement' exists in Europe. (The solitary nature of this desire-type may make it just too incompatible with the notion of collectivity ever to allow for a necrophile-identity politics.)[6] Despite this, the increased tolerance in Western culture with regard to sexual practices and identities has allowed for a certain flexibility in the creative expression of human sexual behaviour. This is accompanied by a greater willingness to accept unusual fantasies, previously designated 'aberrant' within the remit of sexual possibility, a realm which is increasingly seen as shifting, multifaceted and complex. Michel Foucault's seminal study of 1976 highlights the dangers of interpreting this apparent increased freedom to speak about sexuality as straightforward liberation. His assertion that power is discursive rather than repressive suggests that the proliferation of discourses about sexuality in the modern period is as much about the exercise of normalizing power as it is about the voicing of individual desire. I would not wish to suggest, then, that merely to write openly about necrophilia suggests transgression. Rather, an awareness of the limits and uses of existing discourses about sexuality, and a deliberate response to them, can create ruptures in the reading and meaning-making processes.

Two of the most striking examples of this phenomenon are created by women. Gabrielle Wittkop's classic erotic novella *Le Nécrophile* (1972) has been recently republished in the popular *livre de poche* format. This edition brings together Wittkop's self-aware literary portrait of a necrophile's lifestyle and a short essay by F. de Gaudenzi, *Nécropolis*, which reprises the history of clinical observation of necrophilia as a perversion. The volume offers up, rather in the style of a postmodern collage, a series of arbitrary and historically determined 'positions' on necrophilia, without proffering a 'truth'.

Secondly, a recent Canadian film *Kissed* (1996, Lynne Stopkewich), based on the short story 'We so seldom look on love' by Barbara Gowdy, is a sympathetic, non-sensationalist portrayal of female necrophilia. The directorial strategy is one of aligning the cinematic point of view with the principal character, Sandra, in order to avoid the classic cinematic fetishism of the woman's body. Her sexual acts on male corpses are filmed using overexposure and fade-outs, suggesting identification with her pleasure and subjectivity rather than harsh, fixing close-ups on body parts. The aim throughout is to naturalize rather than pathologize unconventional expressions of sexual desire.[7]

The third strand of the necrophilic legacy is very different from that which I have just described. Postmodern cyborg fiction, such as Richard Calder's *Dead* trilogy, takes mythical figures of the Gothic imagination, such as the vampire and the zombie, and maps them onto the landscape of a 'post-human' society.[8] The sexualized dolls which figure in *Dead Girls* (1992) can be seen as the daughters of the beautiful automaton of Villiers de l'Isle-Adam's *L'Ève future* or the bespoke dummy of Jacques's body, which Raoule enjoys in the closing pages of *Monsieur Vénus*. The sexual union of human and machine in fiction of the technological age represents, perhaps, the logical outcome of the breakdown of boundaries between life and death seen in modern necrophilic writing. Where once the largest imaginative leap was between the living subject and the dead other, in such fantasies, life and the organic have been wholly negated, even as states to be overcome. The postmodern subject's ability to desire and identify with the mechanical marks, perhaps, an important ontological, as well as aesthetic, historical break.

Afterword

Throughout this study, we have noticed that the mechanisms of perversion and the processes and aims of representation work in similar ways, in the service of similar aims. The fascination with death and the dead body—in life and art—is explicable as a working through of the invisible and silenced relationship to one's own human finitude. The sadistic and misogynist discourses which have traditionally shaped and characterized such material and—to some extent—become inseparable from it, must be understood as secondary psychological and aesthetic effects: as reflections of the sexual attitudes of a given culture, rather than as prerequisites for the production of such images. The eroticization of death is a means by which the subject approaches the ineffable. Sexuality becomes a template onto which the ideational attributes of mortality are grafted and by which they are vicariously enjoyed. Our unconscious processes its unthinkable relation to death in much the same way as it navigates sexuality, then: through mechanisms of identification with and projection onto the other. What we see in necrophilia is the extreme, literalized form of a structuring fantasy of the human subject. The ethical difficulties of recuperating such destructive and disturbing material are all too real. However, to ignore, to sanitize or to dismiss the very real fascination offered by erotic material pertaining to death is, I would contend, to cut us off even further from an approach to our end that we, as beings in time and space, are compelled to make.

My readings in this book, intersecting psychoanalysis, history and gender studies, have pointed to the way in which artistic or psychological models of thought may be accurate in reflecting the psychical fears and desires of the historical moment at which they arise. The death drive, while remaining a controversial and unverifiable hypothetical construct, is an imaginative model with intense resonance for the philosophical and political period in which it was conceived. The symptoms and effects of historical change are visible not only in the world of political action, but equally in the personal erotic fantasies of individuals and individual cultures. By examining the way in which the destructive impulses operate in the realm of imaginative literature, we are afforded a more intimate insight into collective concerns and beliefs.

Moreover, as my readings of texts by Rachilde have shown, the apparently conservative mechanisms of desire that subtend necrophilic representations may be read against the grain to show up the logic of more conventional expressions of sexuality and to problematize and renovate our understanding of the erotic. Indeed, the model of desire in question offers rich insight into some of the tenets of contemporary gender theory. Notions of plural and shifting identification, unstable gender positions, and the undermining of heterosexuality and genital sex as natural and inevitable are all demonstrated effortlessly in the mechanisms underlying the desire for the dead.

My aim throughout these readings, then, has been to act as an archaeologist of the modern imagination by opening the coffin lid on a series of still taboo images and preoccupations in a selection of literary and theoretical texts. By reading against the grain of psychoanalytic orthodoxy that dismisses the usefulness of the death drive and privileges Oedipus as the foundation of desire, and by challenging much existing literary criticism which either ignores these extreme representations or labels them misogynist, I hope to have offered a revivifying perspective on a pervasive cultural fantasy which is far from moribund.

Notes to the Conclusion

1. 'L'Étrange mot d'...', *Tel quel* 30 (1967), 3–11 (3).
2. James G. Frazer, *The Golden Bough* (1890), and Freud, *Totem and Taboo*, 1912–13 (*SE* xiv).
3. For a discussion of the difficulty of reading politically problematic female-authored texts outside these ideological frameworks, see my article 'Feminist fictions of the flesh(?): Alina Reyes's *Le Boucher* and Rachilde's *La Marquise de Sade*', *Journal of Romance Studies* 2/1 (2002), 51–64.
4. This can be read as a rhetorical political strategy to undermine or subvert the stereotype which sees gay sexuality as intrinsically linked to death because of its operation outside of reproduction. It also reads against the homophobic tendency to designate AIDS a 'gay plague' and, implicitly, a punishment for promiscuity. See also Leo Bersani, 'Is the rectum a grave?', in *AIDS: Cultural Analysis, Cultural Activism*, ed. Douglas Crimp (Cambridge, MA: MIT Press, 1988), 197–222, and *Homos* (Cambridge, MA: Harvard University Press, 1996).
5. Richard Fleischer's biopic *10 Rillington Place* (1971) and Howard Brenton's play *Christie in Love* (1988) are based on the case of John Christie. Works inspired by Dennis Nilsen include a modern ballet, *Dead Dreams of Monochrome Men* by the dance troupe DV8 (1988); a painting, *Dennis Nilsen* (1993) by Dieter Rossi, and Poppy Z. Brite's postmodern Gothic novel, *Exquisite Corpse* (London: Orion, 1996).
6. See, however, Dany Nobus's discussion of the Association for Necrophiliac Research and Enlightenment in 'Over my dead body: on the histories and cultures of necrophilia', in *Inappropriate Relationships: The Unconventional, the Disapproved, and the Forbidden*, ed. Robin Goodwin and Duncan Cramer (Mahwah, NJ, and London: Lawrence Erlbaum Associates, 2002), 171–89.
7. For a discussion of *Kissed* as a film which uses necrophilia as a figure to disrupt traditional cinematic representations of gender and practices of spectatorship, see my article 'Between men and women; beyond heterosexuality: limits and possibilities of the erotic in Lynne Stopkewich's *Kissed* and Patrice Leconte's *La Fille sur le pont*', *Romance Studies* 20/1 (2002), 29–40.
8. See Fran Mason, 'Loving the technological undead: cyborg sex and necrophilia in Richard Calder's Dead trilogy', in *The Body's Perilous Pleasures: Dangerous Desires and Contemporary Culture*, ed. Michele Aaron (Edinburgh: Edinburgh University Press, 1999), 108–25.

BIBLIOGRAPHY

Dates in square brackets refer to the year in which a work was first published, where the edition used is different from the original. In the case of translations, the date in square brackets denotes the year in which the work appeared in its original language.

Primary Texts

This comprises all works of imaginative literature cited and nineteenth-century memoirs and journals. Primary theoretical works of psychoanalysis and philosophy are listed below under 'Other Works'.

BACHAUMONT, LOUIS PETIT DE, *Mémoires secrètes pour servir à l'histoire de la république des lettres*, 36 vols. (Paris: Librairie des Auteurs, 1866).

BALZAC, HONORÉ DE, *Œuvres diverses*, ed. P.-G. Castex and Roland Chollet, 2 vols., Pléiade (Paris: Gallimard, 1990).

BAUDELAIRE, CHARLES, *Œuvres complètes*, ed. Claude Pichois, 2 vols., Pléiade (Paris: Gallimard, 1975–6).

BERLIOZ, HECTOR, *Mémoires* [1870], 2 vols. (Paris: Garnier-Flammarion, 1969).

BOREL, PÉTRUS, *Mme Putiphar* [1839] (Paris: Régine Desforges, 1972).

——— *Œuvres complètes*, 3 vols. (Paris: La Force Française, 1922).

BOSSUET, JACQUES-BÉNIGNE, *Œuvres*, ed. L'Abbé Velat and Y. Champailler, Pléiade (Paris: Gallimard, 1961).

BRENTON, HOWARD, *Christie in Love* (London: Methuen, 1970).

BROWNING, ROBERT, *The Poems*, ed. John Pettigrew and T. J. Collins, 2 vols. (Harmondsworth: Penguin, 1981).

BRITE, POPPY Z., *Exquisite Corpse* (London: Orion, 1996).

CALDER, RICHARD, *Dead Girls* (London: HarperCollins, 1992).

CHAUSSARD, PIERRE JEAN-BAPTISTE, *Le Nouveau Diable boîteux: tableau philosophique et moral de Paris*, 2 vols. (Paris: Buisson, 1798–9).

DELACROIX, EUGÈNE, *Journal 1822–1863* [1931–2], ed. André Joubin (Paris: Plon, 1980).

EBERHARDT, ISABELLE, 'Infernalia: volupté sépulcrale', in *Œuvres complètes: écrits sur le sable*, 2 vols. (Paris: Grasset, 1990), ii. 23–7

ENDORE, GUY, *Le Loup-Garou de Paris* [1987] (Paris: Naturellement, 2000).

FLAUBERT, GUSTAVE, *Correspondance*, ed. J. Bruneau, 3 vols. (Paris: Conard, 1910).

—— *Œuvres*, ed. A. Thibaudet and R. Dumesnil, 2 vols., Pléiade (Paris: Gallimard, 1958–9).

—— *Souvenirs, notes, 1841*, ed. Chevally Sabatier (Paris: Buchet et Chastel, 1965).

FONTANEY, ANTOINE ÉTIENNE, *Journal intime* (Paris: Presses Françaises, 1925).

GAUTIER, THÉOPHILE, *Les Jeunes France: romans goguenards* [1833] (Paris: Flammarion, 1974).

—— *Émaux et camées* [1852], ed. Maxime du Camp (Paris: Conquet, 1887).

—— *Le Roman de la momie* [1857] (Paris: Charpentier, 1888).

—— *Spirite, nouvelle fantastique* [1866] (Paris: Nizet, 1970).

—— *Histoire du romantisme* [1872] (Paris: Jouaust, 1929).

—— *Contes fantastiques* (Paris: Corti, 1962).

—— *Poésies complètes*, 3 vols., ed. René Jasinski (Paris: Nizet, 1970).

GONCOURT, EDMOND and JULES DE, *Journal*, ed. R. Ricatte (Paris: Fasquelle et Flammarion, 1959).

GOWDY, BARBARA, 'We so seldom look on love', in *We So Seldom Look On Love* (Toronto: Somerville House, 1992).

GRAVES, ROBERT, *Complete Poems*, 2 vols., ed. Beryl Graves and Dunstan Ward (Manchester: Carcanet, 1997).

HUGO, VICTOR, *Œuvres poétiques*, ed. Pierre Albouy, 3 vols., Pléiade (Paris: Gallimard, 1967).

JANIN, JULES, *L'Âne mort et la femme guillotinée* (Brussels: Dumont, 1829).

LAUTRÉAMONT, COMTE DE, *Œuvres complètes*, Pléiade (Paris: Gallimard, 1970).

LEMAÎTRE, JULES, *Les Contemporains* [1885] (Paris: Lecène et Oudin, 1887).

MALLARMÉ, STÉPHANE, *Œuvres complètes*, ed. Henri Mondor and G. Jean-Aubry, Pléiade (Paris: Gallimard, 1945).

MERCIER, LOUIS-SÉBASTIEN, *Lettre de Dulis à son ami* (Paris: La Veuve Duchesne, 1767).

MÉRIMÉE, PROSPER, 'La Vénus d'Ille', *Romans et nouvelles* (Dijon: Pléiade, 1942), 439–66.

MICHELET, JULES, *Journal 1849–60*, ed. Paul Viallaneix, 3 vols. (Paris: Gallimard, 1962).

MIRBEAU, OCTAVE, *Le Jardin des supplices* (Paris: Fasquelle, 1899).

—— *Contes cruels* [1898–9] (Paris: Séguier, 1990).

NERVAL, GÉRARD DE, *Œuvres complètes*, ed. Jean Guillaume and Claude Pichois, 3 vols., Pléiade (Paris: Gallimard, 1984–93).

O'NEDDY, PHILOTHÉE, *Feu et flamme* [1833] (Paris: Presses Françaises, 1926).

POE, EDGAR ALLAN, *Works of Edgar Allan Poe*, 10 vols. (New York: Harper, [n.d.]) (vols. i–iii, *Tales*; vol. iv, *Poems*).

—— *Essays and Reviews* (New York: Literary Classics of the United States, 1984).

RABBE, ALPHONSE, *Album d'un pessimiste* [1835] (Paris: Presses Françaises, 1924).

RACHILDE (Marguerite Eymery Vallette), *Monsieur Vénus* [1884], preface by Maurice Barrès (Paris: Flammarion, 1926).

—— *La Marquise de Sade* [1887] (Paris: Gallimard, 1996).

—— *Madame Adonis* (Paris: E. Monnier, 1888).

—— *La Tour d'Amour* [1899] (Paris: Les Maîtres du Livre, 1916).

—— *La Jongleuse* (Paris: Mercure de France, 1900).

—— *Le Grand Saigneur* (Paris: Flammarion, 1922).

—— *Pourquoi je ne suis pas féministe* (Paris: Éditions de France, 1928).

RIMBAUD, ARTHUR, *Œuvres complètes*, ed. Antoine Adam, Pléiade (Paris: Gallimard, 1972).

RODENBACH, GEORGES, *Bruges-la-morte* [1892] (Paris: Marpon et Flammarion, [1938]).

ROLLINAT, MAURICE, *Les Névroses* (Paris: G. Charpentier, 1883).

RONSARD, PIERRE DE, *Œuvres complètes*, ed. Gustave Cohen, 3 vols., Pléiade (Paris: Gallimard, 1950).

SADE, DONATIEN-ALPHONSE-FRANÇOIS, MARQUIS DE, *Œuvres*, ed. Michel Delon, 3 vols., Pléiade (Paris: Gallimard, 1990).

SAINTE-BEUVE, CHARLES-AUGUSTIN, 'Quelques vérités sur la situation en littérature', *Revue des deux mondes* (July 1843).

SWINBURNE, ALGERNON CHARLES, *Poems and Ballads, First Series* [1866] (London: Chatto & Windus, 1898).

VILLIERS DE L'ISLE-ADAM, *Contes cruels* [1883], ed. Pierre-Georges Castex and J. Bollery (Paris: Corti, 1956).

—— *L'Ève future* (Paris: Brunhoff, 1886).

WARGNY, GUY DE, *La Bête noire* [1965] (Paris: Sortilèges, 1988).

WITTIG, MONIQUE, *Les Guérillères* (Paris: Minuit, 1969).

WITTKOP, GABRIELLE, *Le Nécrophile* (Paris: Régine Deforges, 1972).

—— *Le Nécrophile* [1972], with F. de Gaudenzi, *Nécropolis* (Paris: La Musardine, 1998).

ZOLA, ÉMILE, *Thérèse Raquin* [1867] (Paris: A. Lacroix, 1876).

—— *Les Rougon-Macquart: histoire naturelle et sociale d'une famille sous le Second Empire*, ed. Henri Mitterand, 2 vols., Pléiade (Paris: Gallimard, 1960–75).

Critical Works on Baudelaire and Rachilde

Owing to Baudelaire's vast critical reception, this is a selective list comprising only those items most pertinent to the focus of this study.

AUDINET, PIERRE, 'Une visite à Rachilde', *Nouvelles littéraires* 2593 (13 July 1977).

BATAILLE, GEORGES, 'Baudelaire', in *La Littérature et le mal* (Paris: Minuit, 1957), 33–63.

BENJAMIN, WALTER, *Charles Baudelaire: un poète lyrique à l'apogée du capitalisme* (Paris: Payot, 1955).

—— 'On some motifs in Baudelaire', in *Illuminations: Essays and Reflections*, trans. Harry Zohn (London: Jonathan Cape, 1970).

BEIZER, JANET, *Ventriloquized Bodies: Narratives of Hysteria in Nineteenth-Century France* (Ithaca, NY: Cornell University Press, 1994).

BERSANI, LEO, *Baudelaire and Freud* (Berkeley: University of California Press, 1977).

BESNARD-COURSODON, MICHELINE, 'Monsieur Vénus et l'ange de Sodome: l'androgyne au temps de Gustave Moreau', *Nouvelle revue de la psychanalyse* 7 (1973), 63–9.

BIRKETT, JENNIFER, *The Sins of the Fathers* (London: Quartet, 1986).

BLIN, GEORGES, *Le Sadisme de Baudelaire* (Paris: Corti, 1948).

CASSAGNE, ALBERT, *Versification et métrique de Charles Baudelaire* (Paris: Hachette, 1906).

CASSOU-YAGER, HÉLÈNE, *La Polyvalence du thème de la mort dans 'Les Fleurs du Mal' de Baudelaire* (Paris: Nizet, 1979).

CHESTERS, GRAHAM, *Baudelaire and the Poetics of Craft* (Cambridge: Cambridge University Press, 1988).

DAUPHINÉ, CLAUDE, *Rachilde* (Paris: Mercure de France, 1991).

DAVID, ANDRÉ, *Rachilde, homme de lettres: son œuvre* (Paris: Nouvelle Revue Critique, 1924).

DOWNING, LISA, 'Ecstasies and agonies: the "oceanic feeling", God and sexuality in Baudelaire and Villiers de l'Isle-Adam', in *(Un)Faithful Texts: Religion in French and Francophone Literature from the 1780s to the 1980s*, ed. Paul Cooke and Jane Lee (New Orleans: University Press of the South, 2000), 53–66.

—— 'Feminist fictions of the flesh(?): Alina Reyes's *Le Boucher* and Rachilde's *La Marquise de Sade*', *Journal of Romance Studies* 2/1 (2002), 51–64 .

FINCH, ALISON, 'Rachilde and the horror of gender confusion', *Women's Writing in Nineteenth-Century France* (Cambridge: Cambridge University Press, 2000), 206–17.

FISHER, BEN, 'The companion and the dream: delirium in Rachilde and Jarry', *Romance Studies* 18/summer (1991), 33–41.

HAWTHORNE, MELANIE, 'The social construction of sexuality in three novels by Rachilde', in *Papers from the Fourteenth Annual Colloquium in Nineteenth-Century French Studies* [1988], ed. William Paulson (Michigan Romantic Studies, 9; Ann Arbor: University of Michigan, 1989), 49–59.

—— 'Rachilde', *French Women Writers: A Bio-Bibliographical Source Book*, ed. Eva Martin Sartori and Dorothy Wynne Zimmerman (Westport, CT: Greenwood Press, 1991), 346–56.

HIDDLESTON, JAMES, *Baudelaire and 'Le Spleen de Paris'* (Oxford: Clarendon Press, 1986).

—— *Baudelaire and the Art of Memory* (Oxford: Oxford University Press, 1999).

HOLMES, DIANA, 'Rachilde, decadence, misogyny and the woman writer', in *French Women's Writing 1848–1994* (London: Athlone Press, 1996), 63–82.

—— *Rachilde: Decadence, Gender and the Woman Writer* (Oxford: Berg, 2001).

HOWELLS, BERNARD, *Baudelaire: Individualism, Dandyism and the Philosophy of History*, Legenda (Oxford: European Humanities Research Centre, 1996).

HYSLOP, LOIS BOE, *Baudelaire, Man of his Time* (New Haven: Yale University Press, 1980).

KAPLAN, EDWARD K., *Baudelaire's Prose Poems* (Athens: Georgia University Press, 1990).

KINGCAID, RENÉE A., *Neurosis as Narrative: The Decadent Short Fiction of Proust, Lorrain and Rachilde* (Carbondale: Southern Illinois University Press, 1992).

LAFORGUE, RENÉ, *L'Échec de Baudelaire: étude psychanalytique sur la névrose de Charles Baudelaire* (Paris: Denoël et Steele, 1931).

LEAKEY, F. W., *Les Fleurs du Mal* (Cambridge: Cambridge University Press, 1992).

LUKACHER, MARYLINE, 'Mademoiselle Baudelaire: Rachilde ou le féminin au masculin', *Nineteenth-Century French Studies* 20/3–4 (1992), 52–65.

—— *Maternal Fictions: Stendhal, Sand, Rachilde and Bataille* (London: Duke University Press, 1994).

McLENDON, WILL L., 'Huysmans, Rachilde et le roman de "mœurs parisiennes"', *Bulletin de la Société J.-K. Huysmans* 77 (1985), 21–4.

PAGLIA, CAMILLE, *Sexual Personae: Art and Decadence from Nefertiti to Emily Dickinson* [1990] (New York: Vintage, 1991).

RICHARD, JEAN-PIERRE, *Poésie et profondeur* (Paris: Seuil, 1955).

SARTRE, JEAN-PAUL, *Baudelaire* [1947] (Paris: Gallimard, 1963).

ZIEGLER, ROBERT, 'Rachilde et "l'amour compliqué"', *Atlantis: A Women's Studies Journal* 11/2 (1986), 115–24.

Other Works

The following list includes all other works cited in this study, along with a selection of other texts which are relevant to the literary, historical and theoretical material discussed. Again, where translations have been used, the original date of publication is given in square brackets.

AARON, MICHELE (ed.), *The Body's Perilous Pleasures* (Edinburgh: Edinburgh University Press, 1999).

ABRAHAM, NICHOLAS, and TÖROK, MARIA, *L'Écorce et le noyau* (Paris: Flammarion, 1987).

BARTHES, ROLAND, *Le Plaisir du texte* (Paris: Seuil, 1973).

BARTHOLOMEW, A., MILTE, K., and GALBY, F., 'Homosexual necrophilia', *Medicine, Science and the Law* 18/1 (1978), 29–35.

BATAILLE, GEORGES, *L'Érotisme* (Paris: Minuit, 1957).

—— *La Littérature et le mal* (Paris: Minuit, 1957).

BATTERSBY, CHRISTINE, *Gender and Genius: Towards a Feminist Aesthetics* (London: The Women's Press, 1989).

BELLEMIN-NOËL, JEAN, *Plaisirs de vampire: Gautier, Gracq, Giono* (Paris: Presses Universitaires de France, 2001).

BERGSON, HENRI, *L'Évolution créatrice* [1907] (Geneva: Skira, 1945).

BERSANI, LEO, 'Is the rectum a grave?', in *AIDS: Cultural Analysis, Cultural Activism*, ed. Douglas Crimp (Cambridge, MA: MIT Press, 1988), 197–222.

—— *Homos* [1999] (Cambridge, MA: Harvard University Press, 1996).

BIERMAN, JOSEPH S., 'Necrophilia in a thirteen-year-old boy', *Psychoanalytic Quarterly* 31 (1962), 329–36.

BLANCHOT, MAURICE, *Lautréamont et Sade* (Paris: Minuit, 1963).

BONAPARTE, MARIE, 'Deuil, nécrophilie et sadisme à propos d'Edgar Poe', *Revue française de psychanalyse* 4 (1930–1), 716–34.

—— *Edgar Poe: sa vie, son œuvre: étude analytique*, 3 vols. (Paris: Presses Universitaires de France, 1958).

BONVALET, PIERRE, 'De la violation de sépultures', doctoral thesis (Marseilles, 1956).

BOOTHBY, RICHARD, *Death and Desire: Psychoanalytic Theory in Lacan's Return to Freud* (New York and London: Routledge, 1991).

BOWIE, MALCOLM, *Freud, Proust, Lacan: Theory as Fiction* (Cambridge: Cambridge University Press, 1987).

—— *Lacan* (London: Fontana, 1991).

BRONFEN, ELISABETH, *Over her Dead Body: Death, Femininity and the Aesthetic* (Manchester: Manchester University Press, 1992).

BROOKS, PETER, 'Freud's masterplot', in *Reading for the Plot* (Oxford: Clarendon Press, 1984), 90–112.

BUTLER, JUDITH, *Gender Trouble: Feminism and the Subversion of Identity* (New York: Routledge, 1990).

—— *Bodies that Matter: On the Discursive Limits of 'Sex'* (New York: Routledge, 1993).

—— 'Imitation and gender insubordination' [1991], in *The Lesbian and Gay Studies Reader*, ed. Henry Abelove, Michèle Aina Barale and David M. Halperin (London: Routledge, 1993), 307–20.

CALEF, VICTOR, and WEINSHEL, EDWARD M., 'On certain neurotic equivalents of necrophilia', *International Journal of Psychoanalysis* 53 (1972), 67–76.

CAMERON, DEBORAH, and FRAZER, ELIZABETH, *The Lust to Kill* (Cambridge: Polity, 1987).

CARPENTER, SCOTT, *Acts of Fiction: Resistance and Resolution from Sade to Baudelaire* (University Park: Pennsylvania State University Press, 1995).

CASTELLA, GASTON, *Buchez, historien: sa théorie du progrès dans la philosophie de l'histoire* (Fribourg, 1909).

CASTEX, PIERRE-GEORGES, *Le Conte fantastique en France de Nodier à Maupassant* (Paris: Corti, 1951).

CAVARERO, ADRIANA, *In Spite of Plato: A Feminist Rewriting of Ancient Philosophy*, trans. Serena Anderlini-D'Onofrio and Aine O'Healy (Cambridge: Polity, 1995).

CHASSEGUET-SMIRGEL, JANINE, *Creativity and Perversion* (London: Free Association Books, 1985).

COBB, RICHARD, *Death in Paris: The Records of the Basse-Geôle de la Seine, October 1795–September 1801, Vendémiaire Year IV–Fructidor Year XI* (Oxford: Oxford University Press, 1978).

COLEMAN, ANDREW M. (ed.), *Dictionary of Psychology* (Oxford: Oxford University Press, 2001).

CUMMISKEY, GARY, *The Changing Face of Horror: A Study of the Nineteenth-Century French Fantastic Short Story* (New York: Peter Lang, 1992).

DANSEL, MICHEL, *Le Sergent Bertrand: portrait d'un nécrophile heureux* (Paris: Albin Michel, 1991).

DELEUZE, GILLES, and GUATTARI, FÉLIX, *L'Anti-Œdipe* (Paris: Minuit, 1972).

DESROSIÈRES, PIERRE, 'À propos d'un cas de nécrophilie', doctoral thesis (Créteil, 1974).

DIJKSTRA, BRAM, *Idols of Perversity: Fantasies of Feminine Evil in Fin-de-Siècle Culture* (Oxford: Oxford University Press, 1986).

DOLLIMORE, JONATHAN, *Sexual Dissidence: Augustine to Wilde, Freud to Foucault* (Oxford: Clarendon Press, 1991).

—— *Death, Desire and Loss in Western Culture* (London: Allen Lane, Penguin, 1998).

DOWNING, LISA, 'Between men and women; beyond heterosexuality: limits and possibilities of the erotic in Lynne Stopkewich's *Kissed* and Patrice Leconte's *La Fille sur le pont*', *Romance Studies* 20/1 (2002), 29–40.

DWORKIN, ANDREA, *Pornography: Men Possessing Women* (London: The Women's Press, 1981).

—— *Intercourse* (London: Secker and Warburg, 1987).

ÉPAULARD, ALEXIS, *Nécrophilie, nécrosadisme, nécrophagie* (Lyons: A. Storck, 1901).

EYSENCK, H. J., ARNOLD, W., and MEILI, R. (eds.), *Encyclopaedia of Psychology*, 2 vols. (Suffolk: Fontana, 1975).

FELSKI, RITA, *Beyond Feminist Aesthetics: Feminist Literature and Social Change* (London: Hutchinson Radius, 1989).

FÉRÉ, CHARLES, *La Pathologie des émotions: études physiologiques et cliniques* (Paris: Alcan, 1892).

FOUCAULT, MICHEL, *Folie et déraison: histoire de la folie à l'âge classique* (Paris: Plon, 1961).

—— *Histoire de la sexualité*, 3 vols. (Paris: Gallimard, 1976).

FRAZER, JAMES G., *The Golden Bough: A Study in Comparative Religion*, 2 vols. (London: Macmillan, 1890).

FREUD, SIGMUND, *The Standard Edition of the Complete Psychological Works*, trans. from Ger., general ed. James Strachey, 24 vols. (London: Hogarth Press and Institute of Psycho-Analysis, 1953–74).

FROMM, ERICH, *The Anatomy of Human Destructiveness* (London: Jonathan Cape, 1974).

GENET, JEAN, 'L'Étrange mot d'...', *Tel quel* 30 (1967), 3–11.

GOODWIN, SARAH WEBSTER, and BRONFEN, ELISABETH (eds.), *Death and Representation* (Baltimore: Johns Hopkins University Press, 1993).

GREAVES, R., *Nadar, ou le Paradoxe vital* (Paris: Flammarion, 1980).

GUY, BASIL, 'Sur les traces du divin marquis', *Studi francesi* 14 (1970).

HARRISON, NICK, *Circles of Censorship* (Oxford: Oxford University Press, 1995).

HAUSER, RENATE, 'Krafft-Ebing's psychological understanding of sexual behaviour', in *Sexual Knowledge, Sexual Science*, ed. Roy Porter and Mikulás Teich (Cambridge: Cambridge University Press, 1994), 210–27.

HEGEL, GEORG WILHELM FRIEDRICH, *Lectures on the Philosophy of Religion*, ed. Peter C. Hodgson, 3 vols. (Berkeley: University of California Press, 1987).

HEKMA, GERT, 'A history of sexology: social and historical aspects of sexuality', in *From Sappho to de Sade: Moments in the History of Sexuality*, ed. Jan Bremmer (London: Routledge, 1991), 173–93.

HELLO, ERNEST, 'Du genre fantastique', *Revue française* 15/Nov (1858), 31–40.

HENTIG, HANS VON, *Der Nekrotope Mensch* (Stuttgart: F. Enke, 1964).

HOLMES, DIANA, *French Women's Writing 1848–1994* (London: Athlone Press, 1996).

IRIGARAY, LUCE, *Speculum de l'autre femme* (Paris: Minuit, 1974).

—— *Éthique de la différence sexuelle* (Paris: Minuit, 1984).

JAKOBSON, ROMAN, and HALLE, MORRIS, *Fundamentals of Language* (The Hague: Mouton, 1956).

JOHNSON, LEE (ed.), *The Paintings of Eugène Delacroix: A Critical Catalogue: 1832–63* (text), 3 vols. (Oxford: Clarendon Press, 1986).

JONES, ERNEST, *On the Nightmare* (London: Hogarth Press and Institute of Psycho-Analysis, 1931).

KAPLAN, LOUISE J., *Female Perversions* (Harmondsworth: Penguin, 1991).

KENNEDY, LUDOVIC, *10, Rillington Place* (London: Panther, 1971).

KHAN, M. MASUD R., *Alienation in Perversions* (London: Hogarth Press and Institute of Psychoanalysis, 1979).

KRAFFT-EBING, RICHARD VON, *Psychopathia Sexualis* [1886], trans. of 10th Ger. edn. by F. J. Rebman (London: Rebman, 1901).

KRISTEVA, JULIA, *La Révolution du langage poétique: l'avant-garde à la fin du XIXe siècle: Lautréamont et Mallarmé* (Paris: Seuil, 1974).
—— *Polylogue* (Paris: Seuil, 1977).
—— *Visions capitales* (Paris: Éditions de la Réunion des Musées Nationaux, 1998).
LACAN, JACQUES, *Écrits* (Paris: Seuil, 1966).
LAPLANCHE, JEAN, *Vie et mort en psychanalyse* (Paris: Flammarion, 1970).
LECLAIRE, SERGE, *On tue un enfant* (Paris: Seuil, 1975).
LE ROY LADURIE, EMMANUEL, *Montaillou, village occitan de 1294 à 1324* (Paris: Gallimard, 1975).
MCDONAGH, JOSEPHINE, 'Do or die: problems of agency and gender in the aesthetics of murder', *Genders* 5 (summer 1989), 120–34.
MCDOUGALL, JOYCE, *Plea for a Measure of Abnormality* (London: Free Association Books, 1990).
MACKINNON, CATHARINE, *Only Words* (London: HarperCollins, 1999).
MASON, FRAN, 'Loving the technological undead: cyborg sex and necrophilia in Richard Calder's Dead trilogy', in *The Body's Perilous Pleasures: Dangerous Desires and Contemporary Culture*, ed. Michele Aaron (Edinburgh: Edinburgh University Press, 1999), 108–25.
MASTERS, BRIAN, *Killing for Company: The Case of Dennis Nilsen* (London: Jonathan Cape, 1985).
MOLL, ALBERT, *Handbuch der Sexualwissenschaften mit besonderer Berück-sichtigung der Kulturgeschichtlichen Beziehungen* (Leipzig: F. C. W. Vogel, 1912).
MORRA, JOANNE, ROBSON, MARK , and SMITH, MARQUAND , *The Limits of Death: Between Philosophy and Psychoanalysis* (Manchester: Manchester University Press, 2000).
MULVEY, LAURA, 'Death drives: Hitchcock's Psycho', *Film Studies* 2 (2000), 5–14.
NOBUS, DANY, 'Over my dead body: on the histories and cultures of necrophilia', *Inappropriate Relationships: The Unconventional, the Disapproved, and the Forbidden*, ed. Robin Goodwin and Duncan Cramer (Mahwah, NJ, and London: Lawrence Erlbaum Associates, 2002), 171–89.
NORDAU, MAX, *Entartung* [1892], 2 vols. (Berlin: Duncker, 1893).
—— *Degeneration* [1892], trans. of 2nd Ger. edn. by George L. Mosse (London: Heinemann, 1895).
—— *Conventional Lies of our Civilisation*, trans. of 7th Ger. edn. by George L. Mosse (London: Heinemann, 1895).
OOSTERHUIS, HARRY, *Stepchildren of Nature: Krafft-Ebing, Psychiatry and the Making of Sexual Identity* (Chicago: University of Chicago Press, 2000).
PHILLIPS, JOHN, *Forbidden Fictions: Pornography and Censorship in Twentieth-Century French Literature* (London: Pluto, 1999).
—— *Sade: The Libertine Novels* (London: Pluto, 2001).

PICK, DANIEL, *Faces of Degeneration* (Cambridge: Cambridge University Press, 1989).

PLUMMER, KENNETH, *Sexual Stigma: An Interactionist Account* (London: Routledge and Kegan Paul, 1975).

PONNAU, GWENHAËL, *La Folie dans la littérature fantastique* (Paris: CNRS, 1987).

PORTER, LAURENCE M., 'Decadence and the fin-de-siècle novel', in *The Cambridge Companion to the French Novel*, ed. Timothy Unwin (Cambridge: Cambridge University Press, 1997), 93–108.

PORTER, ROY, and TEICH, MIKULÁS (eds.), *Sexual Knowledge, Sexual Science: The History of Attitudes to Sexuality* (Cambridge: Cambridge University Press, 1994).

PRAZ, MARIO, *The Romantic Agony*, 2nd edn., trans. Angus Davis, ed. Frank Kermode (Oxford: Oxford University Press, 1970).

RICHER, JEAN, 'Portrait de l'artiste en nécromant', *Revue d'histoire littéraire de la France* 72 (1972), 609–15.

RIFFATERRE, HERMINE, 'Love-in-death: Gautier's *Morte amoureuse*', *New York Literary Forum* 4 (1980), 65–74.

ROSARIO, VERNON A.: *The Erotic Imagination: French Histories of Perversity* (Oxford: Oxford University Press, 1997).

SARTORI, EVA MARTIN, and ZIMMERMAN, DOROTHY WYNNE (eds.), *French Women Writers: A Bio-Bibliographical Source Book* (Westport, CT: Greenwood Press, 1991).

SAYLOR, DOUGLAS B., *The Sadomasochistic Homotext: Readings in Sade, Balzac and Proust* (New York: Peter Lang, 1993).

SEGAL, HANNAH, 'A necrophilic phantasy', *International Journal of Psycho-analysis* 34 (1953), 90–104.

—— 'On the clinical usefulness of the concept of death instinct', *International Journal of Psychoanalysis* 74 (1993), 55–61.

SHOWALTER, ELAINE, *Sexual Anarchy: Gender and Culture at the Fin de Siècle* [1990] (London: Virago, 1996)

SIEMEK, ANDRZEJ, *La Recherche morale et esthétique dans le roman de Crébillon fils* (Oxford: Oxford University Press, 1981).

SMITH, JOAN, *Misogynies* (London: Faber and Faber, 1982).

STEINER, GEORGE, *On Difficulty and Other Essays* (Oxford: Oxford University Press, 1978).

STOLLER, ROBERT, *Perversion: The Erotic Form of Hatred* (Hassocks: Harvester, 1976).

SULEIMAN, SUSAN, *Subversive Intent: Gender, Politics and the Avant-Garde* (Cambridge, MA: Harvard University Press, 1990).

TODOROV, TZVETAN, *Introduction à la littérature fantastique* (Paris: Seuil, 1970).

UBERSFELD, ANNIE, *Gautier* (Paris: Stock, 1992).

WHYTE, PETER, *Théophile Gautier, conteur fantastique et merveilleux* (Durham: University of Durham Press, 1995).

ZELDIN, THEODORE, *France 1848–1945*, 2 vols. (Oxford: Clarendon Press, 1973–7).

INDEX

The indexing of names mentioned in footnotes has been selective